Americans in
Paris

Americans in Paris

Tony Allan

cbi Contemporary Books, Inc.
Chicago

...right Bison Books Limited 1977
...ghts reserved
...ublished in Great Britain in 1977
...the title *An American in Paris* by
...me Publications Limited
...published in the United States by
...mporary Books. Inc
...orth Michigan Avenue. Chicago. Illinois 60601
...ed in the United States of America
...ry of Congress Catalog Card Number: 77-75713
...national Standard Book Number: 0-8092-7917-7

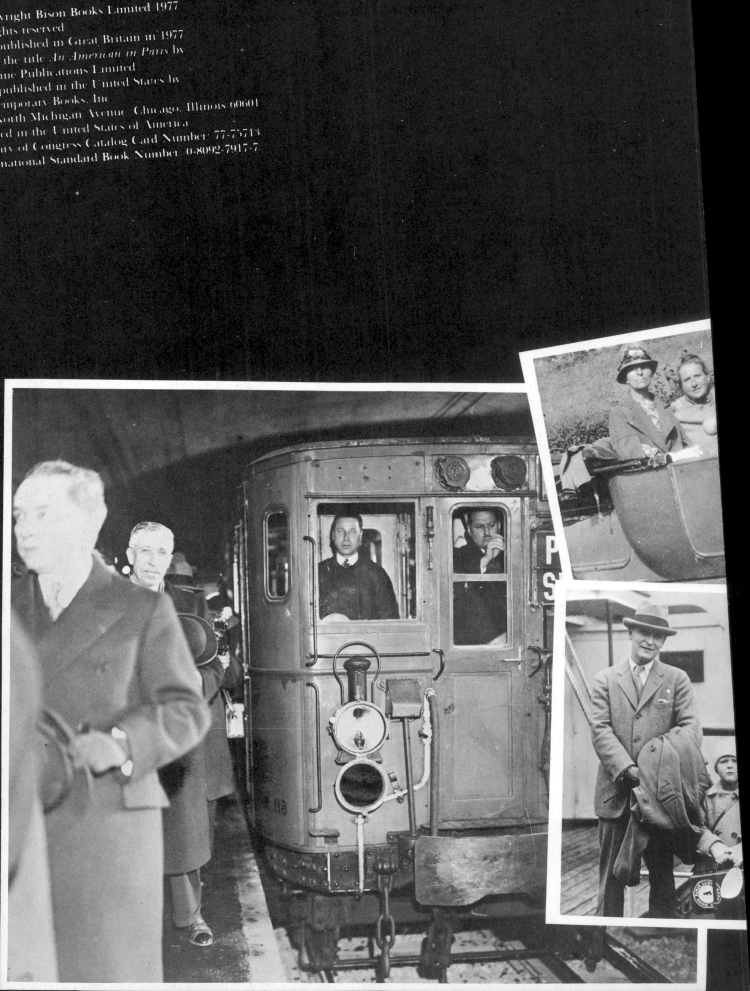

Contents

Introduction
'A Moveable Feast'

For Hemingway it was a moveable feast. Thomas Wolfe called it "an enormous treasure-hoard of unceasing pleasure and delight". The French writer Jules Romains thought it was quite simply "a place and a time without equal in the history of the world". Everyone agrees that Paris, in the two decades of brittle peace between world wars, was a uniquely attractive city. Looking back on it all now, with a retrospect of fifty years, there seems to have been something almost mystical about its appeal. It attracted the wealthiest, the most gifted and the most beautiful people from every nation of the developed world. It was a crossroads and testing ground for all the arts. Schools were founded there and movements born. It was the spiritual, and for long periods the physical, home of Joyce and Proust, of Stravinsky and Picasso, as well as of countless lesser artists whose combined efforts shaped the course of all the arts for a quarter of a century, and whose influence is still felt today.

It was also a tourist attraction on a grand scale. Its hotels and its shops, its food and its women were the envy of the entire world. People who had never heard of Cubism thrilled at the names of Coty and of Cartier. The city's reputation for licentiousness was such that in bars and clubs across America the very mention of its name was enough to produce a knowing wink and a leer. Books were written about it, films were set there, and songs were sung. "How ya gonna keep 'em down on the farm after they've seen Paree . . .?"

Among the Babel of foreigners attracted to Paris like moths to light, the Americans occupied a special place. They were not the most numerous. There were more than twice as many British visitors during the inter-war years. Yet whether because they stayed longer or were simply richer, the Americans were somehow more conspicuous than visitors from any other nation. Even before the First World War, the painter Henri 'le Douanier' Rousseau used to refer to foreigners collectively as *les Américains*. The phrase 'American in Paris' took on resonances that 'Englishman in Paris' or 'Italian in Paris' never shared.

To understand why, it is necessary to make one fundamental distinction between the two groups of Americans who were there: the residents and the tourists. The former made up what would in the nineteenth century have been called the American colony. Not all of the residents had settled permanently in Paris, but even those who were only staying for a year or two tended to regard themselves as belonging in the city in a way that temporary visitors did not. They were fairly cohesive as a group, tending to seek out each others' company. Their relations with the French were generally cordial but not close. The English art critic

Clive Bell had noticed this trait even in the prewar years: "I am puzzled by the persistence with which these fluently French-speaking English and American artists of the quarter for the most part kept themselves to themselves . . . Some of them had French mistresses – kept mistresses; but very few had French friends."

It would be more accurate to talk of groups of American residents in Paris than of one single group, as there were several different cliques and circles, each with its own life style, economic level, and even its own favorite restaurants and bars. There were the survivors of the nineteenth century colony in the expensive streets around the Etoile as well as the artists in Montparnasse. There were American residents in the newly fashionable districts of Neuilly and Passy as well as students in the Latin Quarter and the recently built American House in the *Cité Universitaire*. Yet one thing

Below: *Bouquinistes* (second-hand book sellers) along the Quai de la Tournelle near the Notre-Dame across from the famous restaurant Tour d'Argent.

Left: Flowers offered for sale near the Church of the Madeleine.

Left: The rue Norvins in Montmartre.
Below: Boys sail boats in the Tuileries Gardens.
Right: Swiss cheese for sale in Les Halles.
Far right: A typical *concierge* keeps a watchful eye on the comings and goings of residents and their guests.

Above: The original Trocadero, built for the Paris
Exhibition of 1878, was torn down in the twenties.

that united nearly all of them was the snobbery verging on
contempt with which they regarded the average American
tourist.

This attitude is, of course, fairly common among expatriate groups, especially in much-visited places. In Paris in
the twenties it was aggravated by the traditional Parisian
disdain for tourists in general, which tended to rub off on
Americans who lived there, and also by a sort of socio-
cultural superiority complex which made the residents feel
that they were the trend setters and that the tourists were
benighted provincials trying to get in on their cosmopolitan
act. This feeling grew as the decade progressed, bringing
more American visitors each successive year. "By 1928,"
wrote Scott Fitzgerald, "Paris had grown suffocating. With
each new shipment of Americans spewed up by the boom
the quality fell off, until toward the end there was something
almost sinsister about the crazy boatloads."

Fitzgerald's remark reflects another attitude common to
many of the twenties expatriates: the belief in a Parisian
Golden Age – a time before the tourist hordes arrived, when
only the young, the talented and the beautiful lived there.
In this belief there was much that was simply nostalgia for
the expatriates' own passing youth; but its foundations
nonetheless lay in a bedrock of truth. The tourists were,
after all, attracted in part by the stories of the glamorous and
scandalous lives of the first generation of postwar pioneers.
The concentration of American talent in Paris was probably
greatest in the years immediately after the end of the war –
from 1919 to, say, 1927, by which time the Lost Generation's
diaspora was getting under way.

Not that there was anything new about Americans in
Paris even in 1919. Though the writers of the twenties
sometimes made it sound as though they had personally
discovered the city, there had in fact been a sizeable colony
there throughout the nineteenth century and in the years
before the First World War. There were even Americans in
Paris during the Commune of 1870, when revolution broke
out and the city came close to starvation. They formed a
group called the Hungry Club, and gathered regularly to
dine on such delicacies as cat mince, rat, peas and celery,
and shoulder of dog with tomato sauce.

In some respects the nineteenth century Americans in
Paris had much in common with their twentieth century
successors. There were major writers and artists among their
ranks. The young Henry James earned his living, like
Hemingway, as a newspaper correspondent; he contributed
a monthly Paris letter to the *New York Tribune*. Whistler
spent several years in Paris as a struggling art student.
Another American attracted to Paris by the art schools was
the artist/inventor Samuel Morse. He devised the Morse
Code en route from Le Havre to New York on the slow
journey home.

Traditions of eccentricity and extravagance were also
established early. In Louis Philippe's reign, there was
the aristocratic Colonel Thorne, who entertained the highest
nobility of France in his chateau in Normandy, and who
was reputed to have a finer turn-out than the Citizen King's.
Another wealthy colonel, this one called Swan, chose a less
exalted life style. This comrade-in-arms of Washington and
Lafayette spent the last twenty years of his life in a Parisian
debtors' prison because he refused, on principle, to pay
interest, as the law demanded, on his French debts. He is
said to have slept on a pallet stuffed with gold 20 franc

Above: Two of the last streetcars (trams) are broken up at the Lilas Depot. They were replaced by the *autobus*.

pieces, which he used to buy food and clothing for his fellow prisoners. In his self-ordained confinement he was a contented and popular man. He was finally released under a general amnesty for debtors during the Revolution of 1830, and died, heart-broken, the following day.

Despite these picturesque exceptions, the majority of nineteenth century American expatriates lived discreet, cultivated and comfortable lives – the lives of characters in a Henry James novel. The characteristic that distinguished them most strongly from the Americans of the twenties was their self-effacement. They went to Paris as pilgrims to a shrine, and there was something almost obsequious about the respect they felt for the higher European culture. By the 1920s attitudes had changed radically. Americans still went to Paris as a cultural and intellectual center, but the culture they were seeking was an active, living thing, not a tradition of museum pieces preserved behind glass. They went to Paris seeking a community of like-thinking people, not a communion with the past.

The Americans of the twenties were increasingly self-confident and self-assertive. In their dealings with French intellectuals, the critic Malcolm Cowley noted, "the burden of inferiority somehow disappeared". Several writers have remarked on how odd it was that a generation of creative Americans should have chosen to live in Paris at precisely the moment when, politically and culturally, America was coming into its own. Yet perhaps, deep down, it was that knowledge that made them go. They were looking for a place to prove themselves against all comers. Though they respected the talents of the French contemporaries, the old humility towards European culture was gone. They were American and happy to be it, and in 1920 they were ready to take on the world.

If the challenge of Europe was to be taken up, Paris seemed like the best possible place to do it. It was, artistically, the most alive city in Europe. And aesthetically and socially, a very pleasant place in which to live. Henry James himself had noted that "there is to be found here a greater amount of current well-being than elsewhere." Above and beyond all that, it was – as nowhere else was – an *artists'* city. "If you are a writer you have privileges, if you are a painter you have privileges, and it is pleasant," wrote Gertrude Stein. And Thomas Wolfe, in his own hyperbolic style, added, "So glamorous was the magic name of Paris . . . that I really thought one could work far better there than anywhere on earth."

Writers and artists may have gone to Paris to work and to prove themselves, but the motives of the great mass of tourists, and of many of the residents also, were less elevated. For them Paris was simply fun. It was the international capital of pleasure, the city where the art of living had been raised to its highest point. Its restaurants, cafés and even its brothels were celebrated throughout the world. And in the twenties the hectic animation of its night life reached perhaps its wildest limits.

The city had retained its nineteenth century culinary reputation intact. Such restaurants as Henri's, Larue's and the Café de Paris on the Right Bank, and Frederic's and Foyot's across the river, attracted an international clientele of gastronomes. Yet one of the special attractions of Paris, then as now, was that good food was not the exclusive privilege of the wealthy. The city was also full of unpreten-

tious family bistros where the meals were prepared with love and the bill came to very little. The American painter Stanley Schooner, who was a connoisseur of these establishments, used to advise his friends that three good signs to look out for were a small menu, darned tablecloths, and an old dog on the premises. Mostly, though, he would add, you go by instinct.

The cafés of Paris also took on a new lease of life at the end of the war. To such time-honored establishments as the Café de la Paix, by the Opéra, and the Régence, opposite the Comédie Française, the twenties added new favorites of their own. There was the Wepler in Montmartre, which Henry Miller was to frequent. The *bar américain* became popular, partly to cater to the growing number of American tourists; Harry's Bar on the rue Daunou was the prototype. Most famous of all were the great cafés of the boulevard Montparnasse. The Dôme and the Rotonde were both relative newcomers to the Parisian scene. The Dôme had been there longest, but its earlier history as a seedy neighborhood café was undistinguished. The Rotonde had risen to fame as an artists' café shortly before the war. It was in the twenties, when they were joined by the Sélect and the Coupole that Montparnasse really burst into life.

Every American visitor knew about the cafés of Paris, but the opulence and openness of the brothels came as more of a surprise to those who visited them. The French had traditionally taken a permissive attitude towards prostitution, and by an edict of 1900 Paris's Prefect of Police had authorized *maisons de rendezvous* where prostitutes could work but not reside. By an odd quirk of justice, those that charged an entrance fee of forty francs or more were not subject to police inspection; the wealthy could therefore enjoy their vices discreetly. As a result, the more expensive establishments strove to outstrip each other in erotic inventiveness. Owners built up chains of brothels across the city, and successful houses changed hands, like any other prospering business, for considerable sums of money.

Paris was a banquet for the senses, and it was one that Americans could enjoy for very little money. The dollar was high on the currency market and the franc was low. After the French financial crisis of 1924 the exchange rate, which had stood at seven francs to the dollar in 1919, started to soar. It reached an all-time high of fifty francs to the dollar in July, 1926, stabilized at a little over twenty-five francs in 1927, and remained at that level through the Crash of 1929 and well into the thirties. This meant that Americans could live well on very little money indeed, so long as that money reached them in dollars.

In the late twenties, the cost of a cheap three-course meal came to about twenty cents. Thomas Wolfe has described,

Left: Notre Dame Cathedral and the Seine.
Below: Holiday-makers from the Netherlands arrive at the Gare du Nord.

Above: One of the greatest advertising stunts in history: illumination of the Eiffel Tower by the car manufacturer Citröen in 1925.
Right: How the other half lived in Montmartre.

in *Of Time and the River*, a magnificent dinner he ate at Drouant's – consommé, rump steak, *fonds d'artichaut Mornay*, coffee, and half a bottle of Nuits St. Georges; the bill came to considerably less than two dollars. Even the sexual adventures of Henry Miller and his friends become more credible when you remember that cheap whores offered themselves at that time for less than a quarter.

The fact that Americans could afford almost anything they wanted in Paris is no doubt the main reason for the frenetic pace of the lives that so many of them lived there. Yet there are other, less obvious explanations for all of the parties of the twenties, the wild bar and nightclub crawls that ended drunkenly in taxi-cabs at dawn. They were partly a reaction against Prohibition. In the 'anything goes' atmosphere of Paris, Americans tasted forbidden pleasures with the breathless eagerness of schoolboys breaking rules. Paris was where you could do the things you could not do at home.

In retrospect we can see the twenties as a time of respite. They provided a holiday from the battlefield, a chance to celebrate the ending of the war to end all war. We know now that worse was to follow but at the time the mood was one of jubilation. Americans in Paris could feel that they had earned their fun. For many of them, it was literally their chance to taste the fruits of victory, for the first great wave of Americans to cross the Atlantic had come not as tourists but as the doughboys of the First World War.

Below: A greengrocer sells fried potatoes as well.
Right: The Moulin de la Galette was a pleasant outdoor restaurant in which the waitresses wore peasant costumes.

Below: The rue de Venise near Les Halles.
Right: Some street singers near the Place du Tertre on Montmartre in 1930.

Below: Bathing costume contests in Parisian public swimming pools were always well-attended.

Below: American Legionnaires and their wives returned to Paris after World War I to relive (at least) the gastronomic part of their war experiences in France during the 1920s, when the first great wave of American tourists descended on the French capital.
Right: Artists along the Seine near the Pont Neuf.

1. War and Peace

The greatest American overseas holiday began in the trenches of the Western Front. There had been Americans in France before, but until America's intervention in the First World War they had come in small numbers as visitors or explorers of the old Europe on which America had turned its back. The war democratized the trip to Europe. Among the thousands – later, millions – of soldiers who served in France were illiterate farmhands and factory workers as well as college graduates. In retrospect, the exodus of the doughboys stands as one of the decisive moments of American history. It marked the end of isolation and the beginning of a long affair with Europe; the First World War alone was to cost the nation 50,000 dead.

The doughboys of World War I were a representative cross-section of the country that they served. Despite initial enthusiasm for a volunteer force, a draft was instituted soon after America officially entered the war in April, 1917. Many of the half-million draftees swept in by the first wave of Selective Service recruitment were leaving home for the first time when, dressed up in their Sunday best, they caught the troop trains that carried them away to training camps on the first leg of their journey to the war. Many of them must have reacted like the mountain boy from Danville, Va., who was heard to say, fifty miles from his hometown station, "Bud, if this ole world is as big the other way as she is this, she's a hell-buster for sartin." They were a less sophisticated bunch than their successors in World War II, Korea and Vietnam. Nearly one in three was illiterate. A couple of professors of psychology were commissioned to devise intelligence tests for the conscripts, with the aim of finding jobs suited to each man's talents and abilities. Intelligence testing was then still in its infancy, and the alpha (for literates) and beta (for illiterates) tests that they came up with were undoubtedly inadequate in that they relied heavily on school learning. Even so their findings were surprising; 47 percent of the white conscripts, and 89 percent of the black, were judged by the testers' standards to be below the mental age of thirteen.

Before the doughboys could be shipped to France, the army had to make soldiers of them. After the excitement of leaving home, the farewell dinners and the brass bands at the station and the weeping, handkerchief-waving girls, the monotonous routine of the training camps came as an anticlimax. Like everything else about the war preparations of

Left: American doughboys form a living Statue of Liberty before leaving for France in 1917.
Below: General John J. Pershing arrives in France.

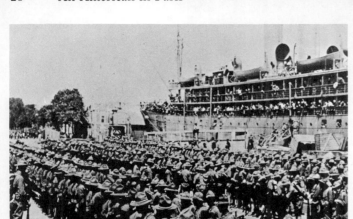

Previous page: The troopship *Mount Vernon* leaves
New York for France in 1918.
Above: The first American troops arrive at St Nazaire.

1917, the camps had been thrown together in a hurry, and
many recruits arrived at their destinations to find that the
buildings they were supposed to live in were only half
finished. Uniforms were in short supply, especially for
exceptionally tall or short recruits, and many infantrymen
did their first rifle drill with blocks of wood. The cold
winter of 1917-18 made life harder than ever, particularly
for men in the tent camps of the south. Life was little
better for trainee officers, who had their own camps.
Reveille sounded at 5.15, and from then until ten o'clock in
the evening every hour of the day was occupied. Yet one
young volunteer at Fort Leavenworth, a Princeton man
called Francis Scott Key Fitzgerald, managed to work
weekends in the Officers' Club and by hiding writing paper
in his copy of *Small Problems for Infantry*, to write his first
novel during his year of training. It was at another camp, in
Alabama in 1918, that as a smart young *aide-de-camp* he was
to make the acquaintance of his future wife, Zelda.

The orders to go overseas meant another flurry of excitement. Again there were farewells and flag-waving as the
trains carried the recruits to their ports of embarkation. For
four out of five of them, this was New York. There was a
final stop at Camp Merritt, where new uniforms, steel
helmets and gas masks were issued. The war suddenly
seemed very near. A few of the embarking troops could not
stand the strain. There were some suicides and self-
mutilations, and about five thousand soldiers deserted.
Many more went away without leave for less than the ten
days that constituted desertion, for a final chance to see
America and their friends before setting off to the war zone.
But most of the troops reacted with curiosity and excitement. The overseas adventure was about to begin.

The trip across the Atlantic was an experience in itself.
The journey from New York's Hoboken piers to St.
Nazaire, the disembarkation port at the mouth of the Loire,
generally took twelve days. Conditions aboard ship were
uncomfortably crowded, particularly in the summer months
of 1918 when the Atlantic Ferry was in full swing and
250,000 troops were making the trip to France each month.
Bunks were in such short supply on the troopships that men

had to sleep in shifts. Submarine scares were common,
though few ships were sunk. The German High Command
had initially hoped to minimize America's war contribution
by using U-boats to prevent large-scale troop movements
across the Atlantic, but the effective use of convoys virtually
removed the underwater menace. In all, less than three
hundred soldiers were lost on the Atlantic. The sight of
British or American destroyers sailing from bases in Ireland
to protect the incoming troopships was nonetheless a
welcome one for the soldiers on board, who were generally
more than content to see the French coast loom over the
horizon.

The first American troops to be seen in France arrived in
Paris with the leader of the American Expeditionary Force,
General John J. Pershing, on June 13, 1917. The reception
that the Americans received was a memorable one. The
authorities had timed Pershing's arrival in the capital to
coincide with the closing of offices and shops in the late
afternoon. Half Paris was out in the streets to welcome *les
Américains*. The general himself, accompanied by Marshal
Joffre and the French War Minister, M. Painlevé, headed a
motorcade of fifty cars that made triumphal progress from
the Gare du Nord to the Place de la Concorde. Last in the
line came a busload of American troops – the first soldiers
from the ranks to pass through Paris. The cars inched their
way down the rue Lafayette and the *grands boulevards*
through crowds that overflowed the sidewalks and filled
the surrounding houses. There were flowers everywhere.
Whole bunches of roses were flung at the general's car. Old
men and wounded soldiers bared their heads as the column
wound past. Women – and at that time in Paris crowds
consisted mainly of women – wept with joy at the sight. The
Americans themselves, who were completely unprepared
for the rapturous nature of their reception, reacted at first
with shock. One officer recounted later that it took an
American in the crowd shouting "Look pleasant, please,"
to make him realize that he had been sitting open-mouthed
and stiff as a wooden Indian. In the Place de la Concorde
itself, General Pershing was summoned by the acclamation
of the crowd onto the balcony of the Hôtel Crillon. There he
noticed a French *tricolor* fluttering in the evening breeze.
In what, for the erect and disciplined commander, was an
unusual moment of emotional unbending, he caught the
flag and, stooping, kissed its hem.

Similarly ecstatic receptions awaited the first actual
contingents of the American Expeditionary Forces when
they arrived in Paris on July 3, and again the following day
when Parisians came out to celebrate Independence Day and
the troops marched from Napoleon's tomb at the Invalides
to Picpus Cemetery, where Lafayette, the hero of the hour,
lay buried. A quartermaster lieutenant-colonel orated in a
manner suitable to Independence Day – "Lafayette, we are
here!" – but for once the old clichés rang true. Franco-
American amity was warmer than it had ever been since the
days of the War of Independence, when sophisticated
Parisians rose from their seats to cheer Benjamin Franklin
as America's representative each time that he entered a
theater. It is not too fanciful to imagine that, long after the
troops had gone home, the horde of American tourists and
expatriates who descended on Paris in the inter-war years
was drawn there partly by half-conscious memories of that

euphoria experienced initially when their country was welcomed by Parisians as a brother in arms.

The shouting and flag-waving soon came to an end, and in a short time the arrival of fresh American troops went unnoticed as an everyday event of the war. Few of the soldiers saw much of Paris. They were usually whisked from the port where they landed to a training camp or to the front in crowded and uncomfortable box-cars with the bald inscription "32 men or 8 horses" painted on the walls. The usual·destination was Lorraine. This rolling agricultural province which France had lost to Germany in 1870 was to be the main American combat zone for the rest of the war. It was there that the troops first came into daily contact with the French, and that the real test of Franco-American relations began.

A certain amount of culture shock was only to be expected. Even the obvious fact that the French spoke a foreign language took some getting used to for soldiers who had never previously strayed far from home. "Doesn't anybody here speak American?" became a familiar cry. Soldiers from farming families found it easier to adapt to the ways of the peasant farmers of Lorraine than did their big-city brothers, but even they were unprepared for the piles of manure that they found stacked in front of each house in the villages. The smell of the *fumiers* as they were called, was sickly sweet and vaguely nauseating for those who hadn't, like the villagers, grown up with it from childhood. American sanitation officers retaliated by forcibly removing the piles.

The question of property was central to the Americans' relationship with their hosts. The army had been billeted

Above: Doughboys parade through Paris, July 4, 1917.
Below: Men of the 64th Infantry Regiment, 7th Division celebrate the Armistice of 1918.

on the region which meant for the officers, having rooms in the houses of local dignitaries and professional people and for the men, sharing houses with farmers or living in barns and stables on their lands. For the local people it meant that the American Expeditionary Force was an army of occupation, even though a friendly one. Disputes over payments for damage done were bitter and prolonged. Householders complained that the soldiers billeted with them treated their belongings recklessly. The doughboys, for their part, smarted at the injustice of the complaints. One private was

Above: Sentry in front of the Elysée Palace. The old uniforms were abandoned even for ceremonial purposes after World War I.

from their boys. Officers were made personally responsible for the VD rates in their units, and sufferers, besides being treated in regimental clinics, were also court-martialled and punished as if for a crime.

One unexpected result of this policy was a diplomatic incident involving no less a figure than the French premier, Georges Clemenceau, himself. Brought up in a culture that had always been tolerant of prostitution, Clemenceau was shocked by what he considered the unrealistic puritanism of the American attitude. He sent a letter to Pershing's head-quarters, criticizing the repressive policy he had adopted and suggesting the opening of licensed brothels for the American forces. Clemenceau's letter was forwarded to Washington, where it found its way to the desk of Newton D. Baker, the Secretary for War. He read it twice, then, reflecting on the effect it might make on the idealistic President Wilson, exlaimed to an aide, "For God's sake don't show this to the President or he'll stop the war!"

In the long run Pershing's hard line was justified by the results. There was less than one case of venereal disease per thousand American soldiers in September, 1918. Drunken-ness was also kept to a minimum, and when accusations of immorality made in an American publication against his troops were brought to his attention by the State Depart-ment, he was understandably angry. The refutation he sent back was only slightly over-optimistic: ". . . Engaged in healthy, interesting exercises in the open air, with simple diet, officers and men like trained athletes are ready for their task. Forbidden the use of strong drink and protected by stringent regulations against sexual evils and supported by their own moral courage, their good behavior is the subject of most favorable comment, especially by our Allies. American mothers can rest assured that their sons are a credit to them and the nation . . ."

Denied the pleasures of the flesh, the doughboys had to find more innocent ways of making contact with the local population. One such way was through the children, with whom the lack of a shared language was less of a problem than it was in dealing with their parents. The kids were eager mimics who soon picked up the intonation, though not always the meaning, of the words they heard shouted out by the American soldiers. One infantryman later recalled how a group of children who lived near his troop's quarters would copy their drill while a ten-year-old leader shouted commands, imprecations and profanities in fine English. For Christmas Day, 1917, the soldiers of the First Division donated 35,000 francs to provide a treat for the children of the neighborhood. Christmas trees were bought for every village in their area, while soldiers in Santa Claus disguises gave toys and foodstuffs bought in Paris to all the youngsters who came for them.

There was, however, a darker side to Franco-American relations, and one of the people to suffer most from it was the poet E. E. Cummings. Fresh from Harvard, he had volunteered to serve in France as an ambulance driver with the Norton-Hartjes Ambulance Corps – an American-staffed body founded early in the war by a Boston archeolo-gist who was then in France. He quickly made friends with another volunteer called William Slater Brown, who had just left the Columbia School of Journalism. The two were soon at odds with their section leader, who considered them

speaking for many when he said later that "We had the feeling that we were over there to help them . . . yet all that concerned them was getting paid for damages." General Pershing was finally moved to issue a special order to defuse the situation: "It should be a point of honor with each member of the American Army to avoid doing the least damage to any property in France."

Even during the training period before the actual fighting began, the doughboys found that life in the war zone was not much fun. To begin with, steady rain, dankness and mud in the autumn and winter of 1917 made a mockery of any visions of a sunny France that may have tempted them back home. Another grievance was the hard line that Pershing and his staff took towards relations with women. Swayed largely by the appalling venereal disease casualty rates in the Allied ranks – the British forces had 23,000 men laid up at the time, while the French army had reported a million cases of gonorrhea and syphilis since 1914 – the authorities had decided to keep the camp followers, who invariably swarm to army barracks, as far away as possible unkempt and undisciplined. In contrast, they became friendly with the French staff attached to their section, and through them with the *poilus* in the nearby trenches. Fraternization of this kind was not encouraged. There had always been an undercurrent of competitiveness in the American attitude towards their allies, and Cummings later recalled his section leader commenting, "We're here to show those bastards how they do things in America." More to the point was the fact that the French army had been plagued with mutinies throughout 1917. The trench veterans were bitter and disillusioned, and American officers wished to keep their men uncontaminated by their defeatism.

Brown made the foolish mistake of repeating some of the stories he had heard from the *poilus* in letters that passed through the hands of the French military censors. The stories, of French atrocities and of soldiers shooting unpopular officers in the back, were exactly the kind of thing to which the censors, after the mutinies, were most sensitive. Brown was arrested by French military policemen, and Cummings, as his friend and co-conspirator, was also taken in for questioning. When he refused to renounce his friend, and also incidentally refused to state outright that he hated Germans, he was sent with Brown to a concentration camp for people suspected of espionage or treason.

Cummings himself has described his experiences there in his classic autobiographical novel *The Enormous Room*. Suffice it to say that Brown and he spent nearly three months in the camp before the determined efforts of their parents, the head of the Norton-Hartjes Ambulance Corps, and, latterly, the American Embassy in Paris secured their release. One of the more heartening aspects of the story was the willingness of high American officials including a Secretary of State and at one moment even President Wilson himself to interest themselves in the case in the midst of a world war. On the other hand, it took three months and the highest possible intervention to get two boys fresh from college, one of whom had no charge against him, out of a French prison. But then, even General Pershing himself was to write later with bitterness of the slowness and stubbornness of the French bureaucracy.

Ambulance service had an attraction for writers and others who wished to see the war but did not want to fight in the trenches. The millionaire poet Harry Crosby saw front line service as an ambulance driver, and was nearly killed by German shells while driving to a field hospital at Verdun. John Dos Passos served with the Norton-Hartjes Corps in France, and later with the Red Cross in Italy. It was there that he met a fellow American ambulance driver, a tall, strapping eighteen-year-old from the Midwest with whom he conversed for a couple of hours without ever exchanging names. It was only when the two met again after the war that he realized that this casual acquaintance was Ernest Hemingway.

Perhaps the most unlikely relief workers in all France were two American ladies who toured the south part of France, first of all around Perpignan and then around Nîmes, in an old Ford car they called Auntie, distributing

Below: American Doughboys near the Arc de Triomphe on furlough from the front.

Below: The rue du Temple and the monument on the Place de la République during World War I.

supplies from the American Fund for French Wounded to hospitals in their zones. One was tall and willowy, the other stout and imposing. Both attempted a military look in helmet-shaped hats and belted, big-pocketed coats, though beneath hers the elder of the two disconcertingly wore sandals, a knitted waistcoat and a shirt with distinctive bellying sleeves. They were popular with the doughboys, with whom the elder liked to join in hearty choruses of her favorite song, *The Trail of the Lonesome Pine*. It would be interesting to know how many of the soldiers later recognized, from pictures in newspapers or magazines, their friends and helpers as Alice B. Toklas and Gertrude Stein.

American troops first occupied trenches in October, 1917, and the first American casualties were suffered during a German raid on an isolated outpost in the Vosges sector in the following month. It was not until January, 1918, that a substantial eight-mile sector of the front was put under exclusively American control. From that time onwards, the reputation of America's fighting men, whom their French instructors had initially considered rather green, steadily rose. Previously the relationship between French veterans and American recruits had tended to be one of teacher and pupil, and the Americans had, understandably, chafed at it. To reduce any possible ill-feeling, the French Supreme

Below: President Wilson and his wife during the Paris Peace Conference of 1919.

Commander, General Pétain, issued instructions to his troops: "French officers should treat the (American) officers of their grade, or of a subordinate grade, as comrades who have arrived more recently than they at the front, and should treat them as little as possible as a master does a scholar. As to officers who are of a higher grade than the French officers, the French should wait to give advice until such advice is requested." After the capture of Cantigny, a village in Picardy, by troops of the A.E.F.'s First Division in May, 1918, such patronization became rarer. When the young Ernest Hemingway arrived in Bordeaux the following month, he was surprised to note the respect with which his uniform was treated; even senior French officers saluted him. It turned out that the Marines had just captured Belleau Wood.

Throughout the summer and autumn of 1918, American troops played an increasingly important part in the fighting. Nine American divisions – nearly 300,000 men – participated in the Aisne-Marne offensive of July and August, fighting beside the French. The American First Army was estab-

Above: Postcard of the Place de l'Opéra. The Café de la Paix, frequented by Americans, is on the far left.

lished as a separate and independent body under General Pershing's control in August, and in September it was blooded in its first independent operation, the reduction of the German salient around St. Mihiel in Lorraine, in which forty villages were captured. Gertrude Stein later told the story of an excursion she made about this time in Auntie with one of her doughboy friends. Each time they passed a cluster of houses, the doughboy would ask her what it was. "A village," she would reply. After repeating the question two or three times, her friend muttered despondently, "Forty villages ain't so much."

In the final campaign of the war, more than a million American soldiers fought on a front which stretched fifty miles from the Argonne forest to the River Meuse. By the time that the Armistice was signed in November, there were nearly two million American troops already in France, with the prospect of a vast pool of untapped soldiery in America waiting to come. It was obvious that the American Expeditionary Force, both by its own fighting record and by freeing other Allied forces to serve on other fronts, had decisively tipped the balance of the war against Germany. America's immense war effort, and the 175,000 casualties suffered by the Expeditionary Forces, had not been in vain.

Or had they? As long as the war continued, victory had seemed like a goal in itself, but as soon as the Armistice was signed, Americans began to wonder again just what it was they had been fighting for. Their country had, after all, no lost provinces to reclaim, like France; her security was not immediately threatened by Germany, as Britain's had been. In the long run, of course, the victory of 1918 was to be incalculably important in revealing the nation's potential on the international stage and in establishing America as *a* – or *the* – leading world power. But that was not why the idealistic President Wilson had led his country into war. The role of conquering hero was one that he found difficult to sustain.

He was more attracted by the idea of himself as an

impartial arbitrator between the warring sides. This was the stance that he attempted to adopt when the peace talks opened in Paris in 1919. On his arrival in France, the President was greeted with wild enthusiasm that recalled General Pershing's reception the previous year. But his relations with the country's leaders, and particularly with Clemenceau, soon began to cool. Though willing in theory to accept Wilson's program for a peace based on democracy and the principle of national self-determination – the famous Fourteen Points – Clemenceau became less enthusiastic when these interfered with his plans to ensure the future security of France by annexing substantial slices of Germany. Wilson's own position as an international mediator was weakened when the congressional elections of 1919 returned a House that was fiercely hostile to him and was eager to avoid any further entanglements with Europe or war. When Clemenceau made substantial concessions to Germany in return for a joint British and American pledge to guarantee France's security only to find that the U.S. Senate refused to ratify the pledge, the cornerstone of Clemenceau's plan for national security was knocked away.

The official friendship between the two victorious allies thus began to melt away almost before the war had come to

an end. Most of the doughboys, too, were glad enough to see the last of France and simply wanted to get back home again as fast as they could. Demobilization proceded apace, and by mid 1919 virtually all the soldiers were back in America. Disillusionment with the Paris peace talks was widespread, and politically the mood was running in favor of renewed isolationism. In many ways the ties that had temporarily linked the two nations so closely had been cut as though the war had never taken place.

Yet the war experience was to have a decisive and permanent influence on Franco-American relations as on so many other things. American attitudes towards France had changed in two important ways. In the first place the doughboys' odyssey had demystified the idea of travelling to Europe. The long boat journey seemed less of an obstacle since two million Americans had made it in little more than a year; France was suddenly less remote. Secondly, there was Paris. For nearly two years France had been right at the center of the nation's attention – and Paris of course was at the center of France. It was Paris that American troops had been fighting on the Marne to protect; it was in Paris that the peace terms were being haggled over, and around Paris that the new map of Europe was being drawn. More than ever before, the city was a focus for American eyes. As the battlesmoke gradually cleared and the scars of war slowly began to heal, a generation that had been sent to France to fight turned its mind to going back again – but this time just for the fun.

Below: A French father with his three grandsons mourns the loss of his son at the Tomb of the Unknown Soldier beneath the Arc de Triomphe.
Right: Veteran of World War I at the memorial.

2. Les Années Folles

On January 17, 1920, France had a new President, a suave political nonentity called Deschanel. He was elected over the old Tiger Clemenceau on the assumption that he would do very little except perform, with dignity, the ceremonial functions of his office. It turned out that even that modest task was too much for him. He soon began to act oddly. While he was giving a speech in the south of France, he made a point which was warmly applauded; immediately, he struck a theatrical pose and repeated it word for word. Shortly afterwards he fell off a train and was found wandering along the tracks in his pyjamas. "You may not believe this," the odd figure said "but I'm your President." He ended his term of office the following year in a mental home.

It was a fitting beginning for the period the French call 'the Crazy Years'. Drunk with peace and relative prosperity, the nation settled back to enjoy the fruits of victory and to have some fun. For the first time, they had the leisure to savor the paraphernalia of twentieth century living. Electric lighting, underground trains, telephones, motor buses and taxis, elevators – all were novelties from the past twenty years. The twenties themselves added fresh toys to the list. The first French radio broadcasts were made from the Eiffel Tower in 1921, and by the end of the decade 500,000 enthusiasts with crystal sets were enjoying the sounds of 'thin air'. While the rich swept the roads in Delages and Hispano-Suizas, André Citröen gave the middle classes the 5 CV, France's first popular car. Citröen was a child of the times. He pioneered American advertising techniques in France, employing skywriters and writing his name in illuminated letters down the Eiffel Tower. His firm made a billion francs a year, but he wasted it all. (In casinos he would gamble a million francs a throw.) He was bankrupt by the time of his death in 1935.

Left: A working class street in Ménilmontant.
Below: Moulin Rouge night club in Montmartre.

The mood of the day was extravagant and eccentricities flourished. While the Dadaists and their Surrealist offspring were inspiring riots, the Duchess von Freytag-Loringhoven was to be seen on the terrace of the Deux Magots in a hat decorated with a large watch and chain. It was the epoch of the gramophone, the cocktail shaker and the nude review. Typists and young workers spent their wages at *dancings* and roller-skating rinks with names like Luna Park and Magic City. CoCo the Clown was awarded the *palmes académiques* by the government, and Dr. Sergei Veronoff with his monkey-gland treatment offered rejuvenation to the rich; he was so successful, according to a popular joke of the time, that his patients showed real aptitude for swinging from chandeliers. Maurice Sachs, France's literary chronicler of the twenties, wrote later, "I remember the decade as a perpetual 14th of July."

The new age brought a new look for women. The days of the long dress and the corset were over. In their place was a boyish style, summed up in the title of a 1924 best-seller, *La Garçonne*. Hair was cropped short, first bobbed then shingled, and bosoms were definitely out. It was a neat, geometrical look devoid of bumps and curves that seemed designed to fit smoothly into the cubist interiors of the day. The older generation, used to sinuous femininity, cried scandal. "Women used to be beautiful and sculptured as ships' figure-heads," Paul Poiret fulminated. "Now they look like little undernourished telegraphers." But Poiret's star was waning and a new name was being heard in *haute couture* circles. With cloche hats, raised hems and lowered waistlines, Coco Chanel carried the day.

Right: Place du Tertre in Montmartre, haunt of artists and poseurs between the wars.
Below: Raconteur at the Lapin à Gill in Montmartre. The harpist Louise Charpentier waits to entertain.

Above: Sketch of Chez Florence in 1926, a jazzy hangout open only in the evenings.

The country was affected with an itch for new experiences and new life styles, and America was one of the places the French looked to for the cure. The doughboys had brought a whole unfamiliar culture to their shores; the French had noticed, and in spite of themselves had been impressed. There was a cult of Americana in the air, but what was admired was not what any cultural attaché would have encouraged. Harold Loeb summarized the attitude of his French friends after the war: "Your intellectual America, yes, it bores me, but that other America of the skyscrapers, of the movies, of the streets, that is admirable." Matthew Josephson's Dadaist friends thought that the true America was represented by the common soldiers, jazz bands, Krazy Kat cartoons ("pure American Dada humor") and above all by the silent cinema.

Hollywood movies were, in fact, probably the most important American cultural export to France. Before the war the native French film industry had had the edge over American films. France, after all, had been the home of the great pioneers of cinema, and in 1913 it had been Louis Feuillade's serials that had packed in the boulevard crowds. But by 1918 the French industry was in ruins, and Hollywood had taken up the baton. The visions and fantasies that French audiences ingested to the sound of pianos or organs in darkened halls were made in the USA, and it was mainly an American image of the good life that remained to haunt their imaginations. "In small villages far from the metropolis," the translator Samuel Putnam wrote, "young French lads were to be seen imitating the slicked-back hair and flaring-bottomed trousers of Rudolph Valentino, while the girls did their best to imitate the mannerisms of Gloria Swanson."

The twenties were a boom time in the cinema industry. In 1922 there were already 42 cinemas in Paris, and the new art was making inroads into the heart of the capital's theaterland. On the *grands boulevards*, where for generations the French bourgeoisie had gone to watch melodramas and bedroom farces, hall after hall closed down to reopen with a big screen and a projector. Other districts followed suit, and by the late twenties cinema signs were adding a new glare to the lights of the Champs Elysées. The cinemas varied in style and quality; there was the 5,000 seat Gaumont Palace

on the boulevard de Clichy or the smaller Studio des Ursulines, a pioneer art house on the Left Bank. But the majority could always be counted on to be showing American films. Douglas Fairbanks, Pearl White, Harold Lloyd and Will Rogers were the stars that French audiences lined up to see.

And then of course there was Charlie Chaplin. 'Charlot' was soon one of the best-known and best-loved figures in France. His popularity ran the gamut from children at matinée performances to poets and intellectuals. Elie Faure compared him to Shakespeare in his humanization of man's conflict with fate. The film-maker Louis Delluc equated his originality with Nijinsky's and called *A Dog's Life* "the cinema's first complete work of art."

Charlie Chaplin has remained a hero to the French throughout his life and has on each of his visits to Paris, been crowned with fresh honors and decorations. In 1921, he was persuaded to attend a gala performance of *The Kid* in aid of war reconstruction work. At the cinemas he was introduced to members of the French cabinet by Ambassador Myron T. Herrick and programs signed by him were sold for F.250 each. Chaplin, however, had agreed to attend on the understanding that he would be decorated. But after the ceremony in a box in the cinema, he was somewhat disappointed to discover that he had only been made an *officier de l'instruction publique*, a rank usually reserved for school-teachers. Over the years, however, the French government more than made up for this slight to his vanity. Aristide Briand made him a *chevalier* of the Legion of Honor ten years later, and after the Second World War he was promoted to the rank of *officier*.

Chaplin's popularity continued in France through the years. It was never to be affected, as his standing in America

Below: A *thé dansant,* where delicate young ladies furtively met gentlemen in the afternoons.

Above: American Indian meets the French on the terrace of the Rotonde.
Left: A crowded evening at *Le Boeuf sur le Toit*.
Right: *La Cigogne* in Montparnasse in the 1920s.

was, by the scandals and brouhahas surrounding his private life and his supposedly Leftist political opinions. The French have always respected the artist's right to be judged by his art, and nothing could have been more repugnant to them than the fuss surrounding the dissolution of his second marriage.

The Lita Grey divorce was a messy business, involving allegations of infidelities and mental cruelty. Perhaps because of his wife's extreme youth, some sections of the American press took up her cause vociferously and a campaign was launched against Chaplin's films on the grounds of the artist's supposed immorality. In some American cities his films were actually banned.

The French attitude to the case was that, whatever the rights or wrongs of the divorce, they remained the business of Chaplin and his wife and had nothing whatever to do with the quality of the films he made. A group of Parisian artists and intellectuals, including Louis Aragon, Robert Desnos, Man Ray and Réné Clair, rallied to his support and signed a manifesto protesting against the boycott of his films.

Chaplin's character of Charlot, so close in spirit to the French mime tradition, won a place in the popular imagination that no other Hollywood actor was to achieve. Yet all the stars had their French admirers, and sooner or later most of them came to Paris. Douglas Fairbanks attracted mobs of well-wishers. Fatty Arbuckle, in the manner of a visiting diplomat, laid a wreath on the Tomb of the Unknown Soldier.

Rudolph Valentino was linked to France by his Russian wife, Natasha, whose exiled parents owned a chateau at Juan-les-Pins. The Italian adventurer, who had arrived in America without knowing a word of English and whose meteoric American career had run from odd gardening jobs through dancing to Hollywood stardom, was already the screen's leading Latin Lover by the time Natasha and he arrived in Paris in 1923. They had come to spend a belated honeymoon, delayed by Valentino's arrest for bigamy. Though he had started divorce proceedings against his first wife, they had not been finalized by the time of his second marriage. The judge at his trial had ruled that Natasha and he must live apart until the requisite amount of time had elapsed.

In Paris the two made up for lost time with some grand-scale self-indulgence. For Natasha there was a wardrobe of clothes by Paul Poiret. Rudolph bought himself twin Voisins, one an open tourer, the other a closed saloon, both custom-designed with steel gray coachwork and sumptuous red-leather upholstery. It was considered fashionable to visit Deauville, so they visited Deauville, travelling there in a two-car convoy. The second car was hired, with a chauffeur, simply to carry the luggage Natasha considered necessary for their brief visit. It also provided a convenient refuge for her when Rudolph's wild driving finally drove her in terror from his personal car.

Throughout the thirties film-stars' visits continued to enliven the Parisian celebrity circuit. Hollywood continued to dominate the French cinema industry after the arrival of the 'talkies' in 1929. The films of King Vidor, Mae West and W. C. Fields were all political and popular successes. A less predictable triumph was that of the Marc Connelly film, *The Green Pastures*, with a black cast; its Negro spirituals came as a revelation to French critics, who compared them to Gregorian plainchant and the religious music of the Middle Ages.

In return, France sent to Hollywood some of its own stage

stars, among them Maurice Chevalier and Charles Boyer. It was not until the late thirties that the French industry again became strong enough to export such home-grown successes as Jean Renoir's *La Grande Illusion*, Julien Duvivier's *Un Carnet du Bal* and *Pépé le Moko*, and Marcel Carnet's *Quai des Brumes* and *Hôtel du Nord* to America for wide distribution.

It has been claimed that the first live jazz heard in Paris was played in clandestine clubs by doughboys waiting for repatriation after the Armistice had been signed. If this is true, then the spread of jazz music in France was spectacularly fast. Within a few years of its arrival, intellectuals were debating it, musicians were being influenced by it, aristocrats were admiring it and shop-girls were shimmying to it. Like the Jazz Age in America, *les années folles* danced to a syncopated beat.

From the start there were two separate audiences for jazz in France. There were those who listened to it, and there were those who danced to it. The first group included a number of professional musicians as well as a peculiarly French kind of enthusiast for whom the music was a field for study and analysis and who could be called the jazz intellectual. The second group was made up of all the students, shop-girls, tourists and others who talked over it in smoky night clubs and dance halls, and for whom it was simply a part of the life style of the twenties, like foot-long cigarette holders and silk stockings.

Of the first group, French composers were among the earliest to note the arrival of Jazz. Aaron Copland designated the early twenties as 'the Jazz Interlude' in serious French music. The composers of the 'Six' listened carefully to it. It left its mark on Honegger. Darius Milhaud wrote his

Création du Monde – based on African legends of the Creation and incorporating many different jazz rhythms – in 1923, a year before George Gershwin wrote his jazz-inspired *Rhapsody in Blue*. Even Maurice Ravel let the new sound slip into his blues-influenced *Violin Sonata* and into his *Piano Concerto for the Left Hand*.

Classical musicians were equally enthusiastic about the new sound. Mezz Mezzrow, on his first visit to Paris, was surprised to find himself giving alto lessons to the double-bass player of the Paris Symphony Orchestra. One of the most loyal fans of the Southern Syncopated Orchestra, which toured Europe in 1920, was the Franco-Swiss conductor Ernst Ansermet. He attended every performance that it gave in London, and later published a eulogistic article about its music. Without knowing the man's name, he singled out the band's clarinetist for special praise, describing him as "an artist of genius". The clarinetist was Sydney Bechet.

The prototype of the jazz intellectual was a wealthy young man of White Russian ancestry called Hughes Panassié. He was one of the pioneer discographers and critics, and in the course of the twenties he was to make himself a one-man propaganda machine for the new music. He built up a famous record collection; wrote about the music in his book *Le Jazz Hot* and in the magazine of the same name which he launched; founded the Hot Club of France which staged concerts, sponsored Django Reinhardt and Stéphane Grappelli, put French enthusiasts in touch with one another, and soon propagated a whole network of international affiliates; and compèred jazz record programs on the radio. In the thirties, when many older jazz musicians were unemployed and halfway to being forgotten, he went to America to arrange recording sessions for them. He even

Le bal de la rue Blomet.

Above: The Bal Nègre in the rue Blomet which scandalized and titillated Paris.

kept jazz on French radio during the Occupation, when it was officially discouraged. His stratagem was to disguise the titles of the records he intended to play by translating them into French; for what censor, checking through lists of proposed records, could recognize *St. Louis Blues* under the name of *Tristesse de St. Louis*?

But it was neither the scholars nor the serious musicians who were to make jazz a household word. Its ultimate success was assured by the dancers, who heard it in *dancings* and cabarets. It was the club owners of Montmartre who were to act as the midwives at its birth, for it was in American-owned night clubs, patronized mainly by American tourists, that the first good jazz in France was heard.

The clubs frequented by the doughboys had operated without police licenses but with the tacit consent of the French authorities. After the last soldiers had sailed home, a few of the owners decided to stay on in Paris and to go legitimate. There was Zelli's, which was to grow into a luxurious and expensive establishment, in the rue Fontaine. There was Mitchell's and Florence's, both run by black Americans – as the famous Bricktop's was later to be.

Bricktop – so-called because of the brick-red color she dyed her hair – was one of the most popular of Parisian cabaret owners. She sang herself, and it was said of her that by the force of her voice and her personality she could silence any argument in the club without missing more than two or three beats of the song she was performing. When Robert McAlmon, a friend of hers, once became noisily drunk in the club, she simply without fuss or malice

signalled to one of the waiters. The next drink he was served was a Mickey Finn. His friends carried him home to bed and Bricktop went on singing.

For all her success as a club owner, one ambition of Bricktop's went unfulfilled for a long time. She wanted to go to one of the grand charity balls at the Opéra. It was Cole Porter who eventually enabled her to do so; he invited her as his partner. Not content with her mere presence at the ball, he made sure that she would be noticed. According to Elsa Maxwell, he persuaded the couturier Edward Molyneux to make for her a dress identical to the one the designer had made for Princess Marina of Greece who was to be the center of attention of the entire gala as a result of her recent engagement to the Duke of Kent.

The atmosphere of the Montmartre clubs was generally far from regal. It was a rough, tough world plagued by protection racketeers and the petty gangsters of what the French describe as the *milieu*. The traditional weapon of Paris thugs and apaches had always been the knife, but in the twenties revolvers became common. Many visiting musicians, retaining habits they had picked up in Chicago and New York, carried guns for self-protection.

One such was Sydney Bechet and his readiness to use his was to get him into rather serious trouble. The incident occurred while he was working at Florence's in 1928. Returning home one morning after an all-night session at the club, he ran into another American musician he knew, a banjo-player from Chicago called Mike McKendrick. There was bad feeling at the time between the Chicago musicians and southerners like Bechet, whom the city boys treated as country hicks. McKendrick asked Bechet to join some of his Chicago friends in a nearby bar, but Bechet, sensing trouble,

Above : A black child dances to le Jazz Hot on a piano. American Negroes were all the rage.

refused to go. It was a banal enough disagreement, but it ended with McKendrick pulling a gun and firing two shots at Bechet, missing both times. Bechet then pulled out his revolver and emptied the barrel at McKendrick and his friends who had run out of the bar as soon as they heard shooting. One bullet grazed McKendrick's forehead, and two of his friends were slightly wounded. But the shot that was to cause the most trouble was one that ricocheted off a lamp-post and hit a Frenchwoman passing by on her way to work.

The whole affair smacked more of Chicago in the twenties than of Paris, and a French judge could have been expected to treat it with comparative leniency as a matter between foreigners had it not been for that unlucky ricochet. As it was, the victim had to be hospitalized, and the court was understandably indignant. Bechet and McKendrick were held jointly responsible, and both served eleven months in prison before being expelled from France. Bechet was not to return to the land where he finally settled until 1949.

From the clubs of Montmartre, jazz radiated outwards over Paris. Its triumph was only partial for not everybody appreciated it. For every enthusiast who frequented the clubs and music stores like the Maison du Jazz on the rue Victor Massé, there was at least an equal number of older Frenchmen who regarded the music as the ultimate in decadence and barbarism. And many young Parisians still preferred the accordions and violins of the *bals musettes*, cheap dancing places where the men had to pay a few *sous*, each time they asked a woman to dance, to cover the musicians' expenses.

It was as a dance music, that jazz finally triumphed. So long as Parisians were content with the waltz, the java and

the fox-trot, jazz was expendable; but after the arrival of the Charleston in 1925, it became *de rigueur* for the capital's bright young things. The demand for American musicians increased as jazz music flourished, and by the end of the decade they were as much a part of the Parisian scene as Italian waiters or Russian taxi-drivers.

In the end, the American musicians became so popular that they threatened the livelihood of the native French musicians. To protect their jobs, a quota system was instituted which officially required the employment of five French musicians for every foreigner hired; in practice, however, the musicians were happy to settle for a 50-50 ratio, at least in the smaller clubs.

The quota created major problems for club owners. Their customers wanted jazz, but there were at that time very few French musicians who could play it with any sort of conviction. Driven to compromise, the owner of one big club with an eleven-piece American band in residence simply paid 55 French musicians to sit in the place doing nothing. He drew some consolation for the wastage involved by reflecting that the total wages of the 55 came to less than half the amount he was paying his expensive foreign attractions. In smaller clubs mixed orchestras became popular. The French musicians would sit out the jazz numbers, then the Americans would retire while the French took over for that other twenties importation, the tango.

Americans always enjoyed playing Paris. "Musicians considered artists, treated like royalty . . . Man, how I loved that town," Mezz Mezzrow wrote in his autobiography.

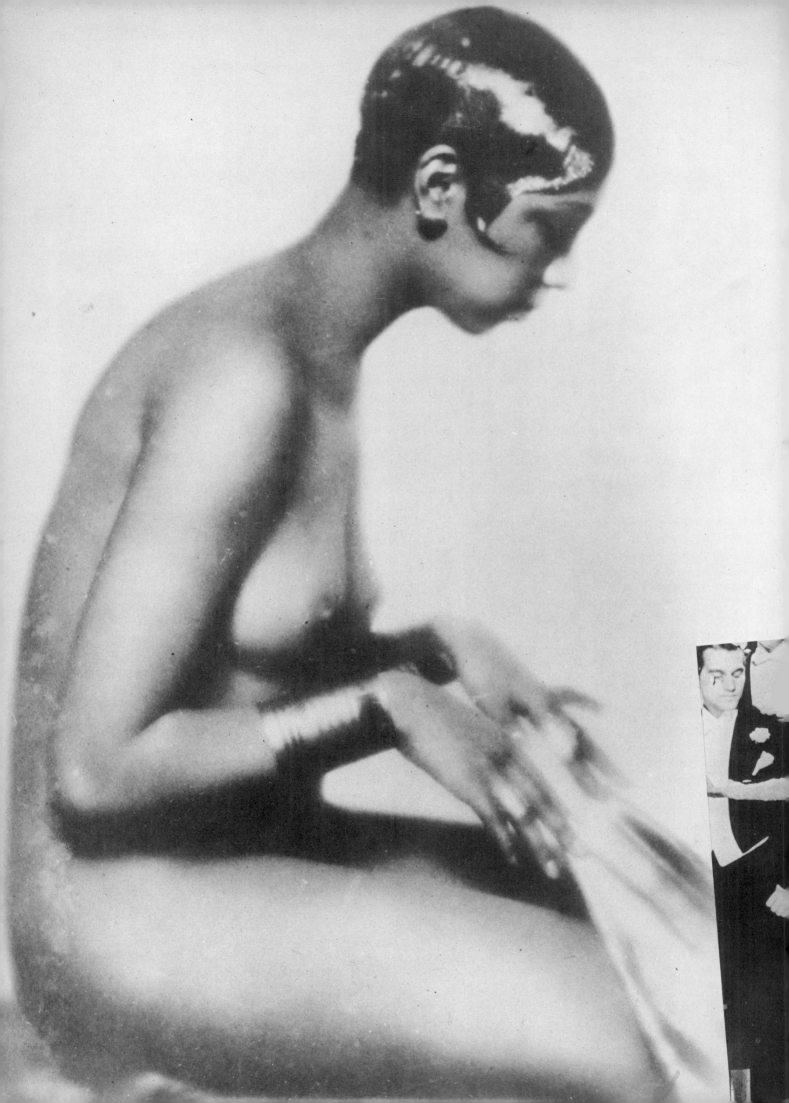

Black musicians were particularly impressed by the lack of color prejudice in France. There was even a certain social vogue for Negroes, triggered largely by a recent fashion for black art. It was a time when the rebel aristocrat Nancy Cunard could embark on her affair with the jazz musician Henry Crowther, and when Princess Violette Murat, dressed up as the bride's mother, could lead a mock Harlem wedding party into a fancy-dress ball given by the Duchesse de Clermont-Tonnerre.

Duke Ellington was particularly touched by an incident that occurred when he was playing the Salle Pleyel in 1933, on his first visit to Paris. His reputation had preceded him, and in the intermission of one of his concerts a representative selection of *le tout Paris* went backstage to meet the maestro at a buffet reception. In the melée, a duchess lost an extremely valuable diamond ring. Musicians and guests joined in the hunt for it, but after a few minutes the duchess called off the search. "I can always get diamonds," she said graciously, "but how often can I get a Duke Ellington?" It was a compliment not merely to the Duke, but also to the music that he represented. Jazz in France had become respectable.

The coming of jazz music was only one part of the discovery of black art. Picasso and his friends had been collecting African masks and sculpture before the war. Writers like Philippe Soupault, Blaise Cendrars and Paul Morand had found material for their work both in the huts of Africa and the streets of Harlem. 'Primitive' motifs were finding their way into furnishings and interior decoration via the Art Deco style, and into Western fashion through the taste for baubles, bangles and beads.

Black, then, was beautiful, fashionable, and sufficiently novel in France to stimulate an audience's curiosity. The popular acceptance of jazz music had turned black culture from an avant-garde concern into a general vogue. Jazz had established a bridgehead into the French imagination. It only remained for black entertainers to cross it, and to win for themselves a place on the music-hall stage.

The great entertainment novelty of the twenties was the coming of the Negro revue. Florence Mills's *Blackbirds* excited audiences in Paris as it had in London and New York. Its star, who had first risen to fame at New York's Plantation Club, was robbed of most of the rewards of her success by her death on a London operating table in 1927 during an appendectomy. She had made no recordings, and all she left behind was the memory of her most popular number, *Bye Bye Blackbird*. Tragedy seemed to haunt that song. It had been the last tune Isadora Duncan had danced before setting off on her fatal car ride in Nice.

The original *Revue Nègre* was staged at the Théâtre des Champs Elysées in 1925 by Rolf de Maré, who had branched out of ballet into chic music-hall promotions. It was the painter, Fernand Léger, who had initially suggested the idea of importing a black revue. An American agent called Caroline Dudley was given the job of rounding up a troupe and escorting them to Paris.

The show attracted considerable advance publicity and the first-night audience included such celebrities as the painters Francis Picabia and Kees van Dongen, and the writers Robert Desnos and Blaise Cendrars. The *Revue Nègre*, which ran for less than an hour, only occupied the second half of the program. Yet by the end of that performance it was obvious that something special had happened. The audience reaction was not unanimously favorable – there had been boos and whistles as well as applause – but the applause was louder and more sustained, and most of it

Left: The lovely Josephine Baker, who took Paris by storm in the mid-twenties.
Below: La Baker and her Boys at the Casino de Paris.
Below right: Josephine Baker and her band clown for the camera.

Above: Josephine Baker as she appeared in her Parisian debut in 1925.

Above: Baker and her black troupe appear at the Exposition Coloniale in 1931.

was directed at the show's previously unknown star, a 19-year-old girl from St. Louis called Josephine Baker.

For years to come she was to be the most talked-about woman in Paris. She was the Ebony Venus, whose frenzied dancing and sinuous, naked beauty gave jaded Parisian audiences a fresh image of sexuality. One critic wrote that "she gave eroticism style"; another compared her to the black Aphrodite who had haunted Baudelaire.

Both her admirers and her detractors regarded her simply as a beautiful, sensuous animal. For her detractors, her appeal was barbarous and demoralizing; for the admirers she was a seductive reincarnation of the Noble Savage, radiating a natural healthy sex appeal uncontaminated by Parisian coquetry.

The irony of it all was that by birth she was half European. Her real father was a Spaniard her mother had known in St. Louis. The couple had been prevented from marrying by the Spaniard's family, and the mother subsequently married a black American. Josephine was born within a few months of the marriage. The light tan coloration that was to delight European audiences had earlier differentiated her from the other children of her neighborhood in St. Louis. She was a mulatto.

Below: Baker appearing in a cabaret performance.

Her upbringing, however, was 'black American' of the most deprived kind. The family of six often had to live in a single room. They rarely had enough to eat, and one of Josephine's memories of her childhood was of looking for scraps of food in the ash-cans of wealthy neighborhoods. The prize pickings were spoiled vegetables and chicken heads for making stock. At the age of seven the young girl was sent to work for a wealthy but sadistic white woman who, when she cracked some dishes, punished her by plunging her hands into boiling water. Josephine was sent home, and her tormenter was arrested.

Show business was Josephine's escape-route from poverty. As a child, she entertained her friends with impromptu acts performed on improvised stages. When she was thirteen, a travelling burlesque troupe called the Dixie Steppers played the black theater in her neighborhood. Pretending to be fifteen, she talked her way into a job with them, and left home without her parents' knowledge.

She started her stage career as a comic, not a beauty. Her greatest talent was for crossing her eyes and pulling faces. It was as the funny girl of the chorus line that she got her first real break, in Sissle and Blake's pioneer black reviews and at the Plantation Club. Yet in America she was never regarded as star material. When she was hired to go to France with the *Revue Nègre*, it was not as the leading attraction – that was to be the red hot mamma Maud de Forest – but as one of 24 supporting musicians and dancers.

It took very little time, though, for the Parisian director to decide that what the French audience wanted was Josephine Baker. To the chagrin of the rest of the chorus, he singled her out for the solo dancing spots. From the moment of her first-night entrance, spreadeagled upside down over an actor's shoulders and entirely naked but for a miniature skirt of flamingo feathers, it was obvious that his judgment had been vindicated. By the end of her first performance in Paris she was a star.

For the next fifteen years she was to enjoy an almost unbroken sequence of successes. The *Revue Nègre* had created her reputation as the naked dancer who introduced the Charleston to Paris. She bolstered that image at the

LA
REVUE NÈGRE
AU
Music-hall
DES
CHAMPS-ÉLYSÉES
PAUL COLIN
H. CHACHOIN Imp. PARIS - 1925

Le restaurant de la mosquée

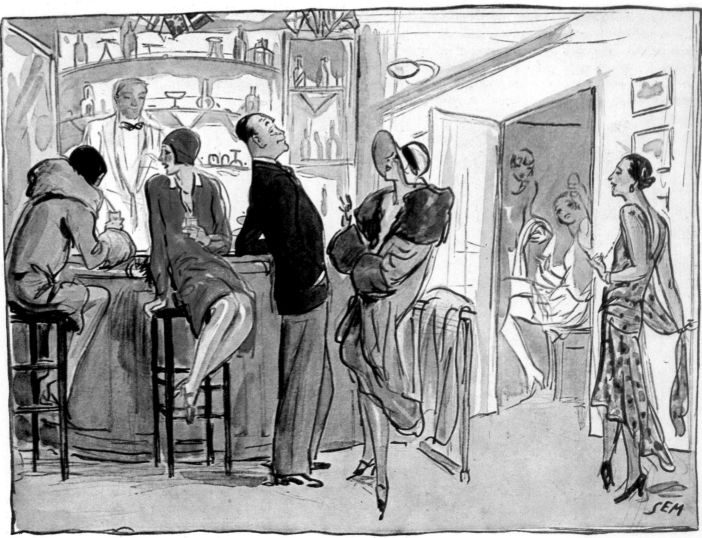

Cie Gle TRANSATLANTIQUE
French Line
Hâvre,
Plymouth,
New-York.

NORMANDIE

French Line

E HAVRE – SOUTHAMPTON – NEW-YORK

Le Lido.

La douloureuse

Le restaurant chinois

Le bar du Czaklir.

Le bal de la rue Blom

Chez les Wikings

Les Montparnot

ROGER
BRODERS

VICHY
COMITÉ DES FÊTES

Office PRIMO. 7. Rue Jean Jaurès. Vichy

LUCIEN SERRE & Cⁱᵉ PARIS.

Below: Baker's feathered finery gilded the demure and talented star.

Folies Bergère, where she danced in her famous skirt of bananas – sixteen of them, slung suggestively about her haunches. There were tours of central Europe, of Scandinavia and of South America, on which she created scandals and made headlines. At the Casino de Paris in 1930 she performed in a more sophisticated cabaret acting passably well in a number of sketches and revealing herself as a talented singer with her first and greatest hit, *J'ai deux amours*.

In the course of the thirties she was to star in a couple of French-made films; in one she played opposite Jean Gabin, she also ventured into light opera as the heroine of Offenbach's *La Créole*. The only upset in her triumphal progress came on a return visit to America, when she flopped the in Ziegfeld Follies.

In France her position was now unchallengeable. Everything about her was newsworthy: her gold fingernails, which led Anna de Noailles to christen her "the pantheress with golden claws"; her leopard, Chiquita, for which she bought a different collar to match each of her dresses; her snakeskin-upholstered Delage limousine; her fur wraps and her jewels. Women imitated her close-cropped slicked-down hairstyle, and bought trademarked products *pour se bakerfixer les cheveux*. At Deauville a whole vogue for sunbathing was created by women trying to emulate her caramel skin color.

Her male admirers were even more fanatical. A *soi-disant* Italian count gave up his job, his family and his country to become her manager. A young French aristocrat followed her on tour through France, Belgium and England, sending red roses backstage after every performance. He eventually ended up in an asylum, and only recovered his wits after Josephine had been persuaded to go and visit him. In Budapest a young Hungarian who had attended her cabaret performance every night for the three weeks of her stay performed the supreme act of devotion by pulling out a pistol at the end of her final performance and shooting himself.

Josephine had only one American rival in the Paris show-business world. For a few years in the late twenties, a trapeze and high-wire artist called Barbette became the talk of the town. Barbette attracted the cream of Parisian society to the Cirque Médrano, the Empire and the Casino de Paris. Costumes made from fifty pounds of ostrich plumes and a finale which included a splendid Icarus-like fall to the safety net certainly made for good showmanship, but the real climax of Barbette's act came at the end of the performance, when the star pulled off a blonde wig to reveal a man's head. Barbette was in fact a young Texan male whose real name was Vander Clyde.

In those days drag acts were rare, and Barbette was considered very daring. Jean Cocteau, who idolized him, teased Josephine Baker by telling her that Barbette was her opposite: "He conceals everything, you reveal everything." Maurice Sachs, his ears always pricked for scandal, went to visit the young star in his hotel room. He found a naked figure lying on the bed with his face covered in black pomade. A book was lying on the table by the bedside; its title was *L'Onanisme seul et a deux*.

Cocteau was also to champion another unlikely American entertainer in Paris. He was the boxer Panama Al Brown, world bantamweight champion for six years. In 1938, Brown was hired to do a song-and-dance act at the Cirque Médrano. Cocteau supplied program notes, describing him as "a phantom, a shadow, more terrible than lightning and the cobra". As an entertainer the audience found him just plain terrible. He had better luck in the ring – he won his Paris bout.

Other entertainers came and went, but Josephine Baker's

Left: Her talents made her a star in Paris overnight.
Below: Baker's comic qualities matched her beauty.

career just seemed to go on and on. Amazingly enough, she retained amid all the adulation not only her sanity but also an attractive innocence. She disliked books and was never to be corrupted by the fruit of the tree of knowledge. In actual fact, she was ignorant. She had never heard of Albert Einstein, and on being introduced to him wondered who he was. When first asked if she would like to perform in an Offenbach operetta, she wanted to know if M. Offenbach wanted her for the part. Offenbach had of course died more than half a century before.

Yet she made up for what she lacked in knowledge by the 'rightness' of her instincts. She was the archetypal showgirl with a heart of gold. She adored children (the loss of her only baby caused the break-up of her brief first marriage) and surrounded herself with a small zoo of animals. She could be impulsively generous, and cried easily. She was a fervent defender of good causes. She spoke at meetings of France's League against Racism and Anti-semitism, and was one of the first stars to rally to de Gaulle.

The apotheosis of her sentimental humanism was the 'rainbow tribe' of orphans of different colors, creeds and nationalities that she and her second husband, a French bandleader, gathered at their chateau in the Dordogne after the Second World War. There were eventually twelve of them, from countries as far apart as Algeria, Canada, Colombia, Finland and Japan. The family was the great concern of her final years. To support it in the face of mounting debts, she was forced at the age of sixty to return to the stage. Her final triumphs were perhaps the sweetest of her life, for with the money earned from her performances the family was saved – at heart the Ebony Venus had always been an Earth-mother.

Below and right: Baker's elegance did not disguise her ingénue qualities. She was a dynamic and elegant star.

3. The Salons

As the last doughboys waited for demobilization, two of the odder residents of Paris's sixth arrondissement resumed lives that the war had inconvenienced but not disrupted. They were both American women who had made their mark in the city before the war began, and who could already claim a distinguished and talented circle of friends. Their two salons may have been unconventional by traditional standards, but insofar as they provided meeting places for creative minds, the houses played their part in a Parisian tradition that dated back three hundred years.

Gertrude Stein and Natalie Clifford Barney both came from wealthy backgrounds and lived in Paris on private means. Both had literary ambitions and had published books. And both were Lesbians who had come to Paris as young women to live their lives in an atmosphere of tolerance they could not then have found at home. Yet despite many similarities, the two were poles apart in taste and temperament. While Stein lived a life of contented monogamy with Alice B. Toklas, Barney was an ardent womanizer, given to passionate romantic attachments with a number of different partners. Barney chose to consider herself French, but Stein remained so close to her native land that, after almost forty years of life in exile, she could still bark at a reporter, "Don't you dare call me an expatriate – I am more American than you could ever hope to be." And if Barney's world was tinged with *fin-de-siècle* aestheticism, Stein was to make her reputation as the high priestess of the modern.

Gertrude Stein was the older of the two. Born in 1870, she was the daughter of a peripatetic businessman of German Jewish stock who ended his career as vice-president of a street railway company in San Francisco. After his death the sale of the franchise on the railway and of some property provided his children with a regular remittance that amounted, in the years before World War I, to about $150 a month. This was not a great deal of money even then though the Steins' artist friends, who had much less, regarded them as little short of millionaires. Yet it did provide the funds for the Stein collections of modern art. Later, Gertrude was to advise Hemingway that the way to build a picture collection is to buy the work of young painters of the same age as oneself and to save money for paintings by economizing on clothes.

After studying under William James at Radcliffe, Gertrude decided to become a doctor and entered the Johns Hopkins Medical School. But she had mistaken her vocation, and after four not very happy years there she dropped out. It was at this time that her brother Leo exercised a decisive influence on her life. He decided, in 1903, to move to Paris to live as an artist. It was Leo who discovered and first rented the apartment that she was to make famous at 27 rue de Fleurus.

Leo Stein was to give up art almost as quickly as Gertrude gave up medicine. He was bearded and balding, an intellectual who had, to an even greater degree than his sister, a taste for theorizing. He had what was probably a finer, more critical intelligence than Gertrude's, but lacked her qualities of dogged persistence and originality. His ideas and discoveries always had a familiar ring about them; the art critic Bernard Berenson called him a man who was always inventing the umbrella. Yet he was to shape the course of his sister's life, first by encouraging her to join him in Paris, and then by introducing her to the work of Cézanne, and through Cézanne to modern painting. It was Leo who, against Gertrude's wishes, bought the first of the Stein Picassos.

The paintings that the brother and sister bought in their first years in Paris provided the foundation on which Gertrude's later reputation as the sybil of the avant-garde was built. In 1904 they were buying Cézannes, Gauguins, Renoirs and a Toulouse-Lautrec. In 1905 they pulled off a major coup with the discovery of Matisse. They bought his *Woman with a Hat* from that year's Salon, where the painting had been generally ridiculed. In the same year the first Picasso joined the collection, and Gertrude, despite her initial displeasure, was soon a more ardent supporter of the young Spaniard's work than her brother.

The Steins befriended both Picasso and Matisse. They offered them hospitality and praise at a point in their careers when these blessings were in short supply. Soon the two were regular visitors to the Saturday evening gatherings at the rue de Fleurus, where painters, informed art-lovers

Left: Gertrude Stein in her atelier in the rue de Fleurus, with Picasso's famous portrait above her.
Below: Alice B. Toklas and Stein on a country outing.

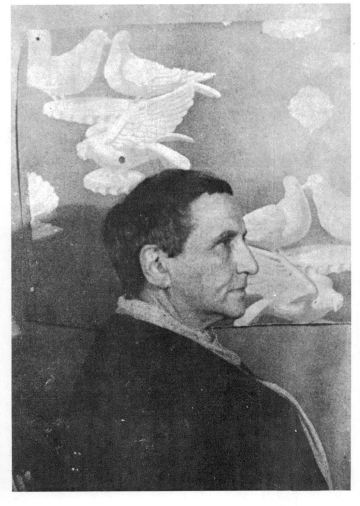

and the simply curious came to look at the paintings and talk about art. One of the ways in which Gertrude endeared herself to Picasso was by saving the comic pages from her American newspapers for him; he was particularly fond of the Katzenjammer Kids. Picasso liked to surround himself with a protective group of friends and it was in this way that Braque and the poets, Guillaume Apollinaire and Max Jacob, entered the Stein circle. Despite the 'defection' of Picasso when Stein moved from Montmartre before World War I, her circle continued to widen.

The Stein collection quickly attracted the attention of a small group of American modernist painters who made a point of dropping in to look at it whenever they found themselves in Paris: Gertrude Stein developed something of an underground reputation in America. By the time the new art was publicly revealed to a shocked and amused New York at the Armory Show of 1913, her name was already associated with it. Thus, a little of the enormous publicity that the show received rubbed off on the strange young woman who lived in the Fauvists' very lair, and who was known to produce incomprehensible writings that newspapers liked to consider as Cubist. By the time that the show closed, the media's mockery had made her a minor celebrity.

By that time Alice B. Toklas had entered her life, and Leo had all but left it. Alice, the 29-year-old daughter of a San Francisco property owner, had come to Paris in 1907 for what was intended to be a short visit. She had met Gertrude's elder brother, Michael, in San Francisco earlier. He was living in Paris also, avidly collecting Matisses, and it was at his flat that Alice first met Gertrude. The two women fell in love with each other almost immediately, with Gertrude taking the initiative in the relationship from the start. For reasons of propriety, nearly three years passed before Alice eventually moved into the apartment in the rue de Fleurus. At first, Leo accepted the new arrangement equably, but a rift had been created that gradually widened. He finally left in 1913 to live in Italy, taking the Renoirs and all but one of the Matisses with him. Gertrude's share of their joint collection included all the Picassos.

When Gertrude returned to Paris after the war – her final posting with the American Fund for French Wounded had been in Alsace – she went back to an established reputation as a collector of modern art and to a lesser notoriety as a writer of eccentric prose pieces that many people had heard of but few had read. She had published her first book, *Three Lives*, at her own expense in 1908; in the first eighteen months of publication it sold 73 copies. In the wake of her Armory Show publicity a New York publisher had brought out a collection of more experimental writings that she had entitled *Tender Buttons*. Again sales had been limited, and she was to remain nobody's idea of a popular author until the success of the deceptively-titled *Autobiography of Alice B. Toklas*, a book that says little about Miss Toklas and much about its real author Miss Stein, in 1933.

In 1919, then, she was an imposing 45-year-old with a commanding personality and a great deal of physical

Left: Two portraits of Gertrude Stein. Her prose and poetry were as complex as she was.

presence. She was big-boned and broad-framed, and the contrast between her stout, heavy-set figure and the slim, gypsy-like fragility of Alice Toklas was piquant. Her taste in dress was as original as her taste in writing. At this stage of her life she was affecting oriental sandals with pointed toes and a hat that one observer called "a most becoming top of a basket". Hemingway, who first met her in 1922, thought that she looked then like "a northern Italian peasant woman", and wrote appreciatively of "her lovely thick, alive, immigrant hair which she wore put up in the same way she had probably worn it in college". It was four years later that she first adopted the butch, close-cropped style of her later years which, Hemingway noted disapprovingly, made her look like a Roman emperor. But by that time their friendship had, for more serious reasons, already begun to cool.

Her old friends had been scattered by the war. Matisse had moved to Nice. Picasso had married a Russian ballerina and under her influence he was living a sedate Right Bank life and saw little of his old friends. Guillaume Apollinaire, who had done so much to hold the Picasso circle together, was dead, a victim of the postwar Spanish flu epidemic. The story goes that as he lay dying in his apartment on the boulevard Saint Germain he heard the crowds howling for the Kaiser's blood with shouts of "*A bas Guillaume*", and in his delirium had thought that it was his own death they were awaiting.

Yet the prospect of losing friends never greatly worried Gertrude Stein. She was famous enough by this time to expect and to receive a constant stream of new visitors. She enjoyed new faces and used to say that she liked to see people come but, just as much, she liked to see them go. She did not have long to wait for the first arrivals. Strangers would appear at her door, armed with a letter of introduction or merely with news of a mutual friend. They were usually received hospitably, though when Gertrude was busy with her writing Alice would be sent to arrange an audience for a more convenient time.

Some things had changed since the early days. The Saturday evenings had been discontinued as an economy measure. The visitors, who now came at irregular hours throughout the week at Gertrude's invitation, were also different. There were fewer painters and more writers. The percentage of French guests was smaller and the number of Americans had grown. One of the first to arrive was Ezra Pound, whom Gertrude had met at the home of an American friend. Perhaps because they were both people of fixed and dogmatic opinions, her relations with the poet were never very easy, and ended altogether after Pound, in the heat of a discussion, crippled an armchair of which Stein and Toklas were both very fond. She later wrote of him that he was "a village explainer, excellent if you were a village . . .".

She formed a firmer friendship with the writer Sherwood Anderson, who had the tact to oil their relationship with a constant stream of flattery. It was Anderson who engineered the first meeting between Stein and Ernest Hemingway. Hemingway, then 23, was at first greatly impressed by the cosmopolitan charm of the older woman, whose writings he admired. He arranged for the publication of her massive novel, *The Making of Americans*, in serial form in the *transatlantic review*, and ensured that she received every

possible cent for it. In return, Gertrude gave him advice on his writing and on life in Europe – it was she who first aroused his interest in bull-fighting – and agreed, with Alice Toklas, to be a godmother to his first child.

Other new friends of this time were the artist and photographer Man Ray, the writers Robert McAlmon, Djuna Barnes and Mina Loy, and, among her French visitors, Jean Cocteau and Jacques Lipschitz. They were entertained in the studio, a large room furnished mainly with antique Italian pieces whose solid traditionalism contrasted with the innovatory works of art the room contained. Gertrude received her guests enthroned on a Renaissance chair or else reclining full-length on a divan. They were served tea or liqueurs distilled from fruits – mirabelles, framboises and quetsches. They could admire the Cubist paintings on the walls, where Juan Gris canvases had now joined the Picassos. Most of their attention, however, was generally held by their hostess, who talked animatedly, with some hesitation and repetition, of her theories on life and art and of her own writings. For some of her listeners there was something almost naive about her sophomoric greed for intellectualizing, but most were charmed by her spontaneity and lack of affectation. It was only towards the end of her life that her self-certainty passed reasonable bounds and that she started referring to herself in public as a genius. She had, perhaps, by that time received too many compliments.

Friends came and went throughout the twenties and thirties, but the relationship with Alice B. Toklas remained. In public at least, Alice was content to play a subordinate role. She was part lady's companion, part priestess in the Temple of Stein, organizing the details of daily life at the rue de Fleurus and shielding Gertrude from boring or troublesome visitors. She had the duty of entertaining the wives of famous guests, and she would sit talking to them of household matters and favorite recipes, discreetly but firmly preventing them from participating in the *tête-à-tête* between Gertrude and their husbands. If these wifely conversations became noisy or intrusive, Gertrude was not above shouting at Alice to keep quiet, whereupon Alice would retreat into a pointed and sulky silence for the rest of the visit. About their emotional relationship the two maintained a discreet silence that no outsider was ever tactless enough to question. Yet occasional asides in Gertrude's voluminous writings reveal the depth of her affection for Alice. In private, Gertrude was 'Lovey' and Alice 'Pussy'.

The thirties were to be a good decade for the two of them. They had in 1929 finally succeeded in renting a country house that they had long coveted at Bilignin in the Ain, a quiet rural *département* in eastern France. For several years previously they had spent their summers at a hotel in nearby Belley, the departmental capital. Belley, said Gertrude Stein, did not belie its name. It had been the home of the celebrated nineteenth century gastronome, Brillat-Savarin, and the tradition of good cooking in the region had not died.

From 1929 onwards the couple spent the summer months at Bilignin, and it was there that they were to spend the first years of World War 2. Alice came into her own at Bilignin, occupying herself with the kitchen, the vegetable garden, and the care of Basket, their poodle, or else making preparations for the steady stream of guests they received each year.

Gertrude rose late each morning, and spent her days walking in the neighboring countryside or simply writing and thinking. "It takes a lot of time to be a genius," she wrote, "you have to sit around so much doing nothing."

It was also at this time that Gertrude's career as a writer came to some sort of fruition. Though she was never prepared to admit it, her life had been her most significant work of art, and it was only when she set out to write about it that she finally achieved the kind of recognition that she had always craved. *The Autobiography of Alice B. Toklas* was both a critical and a commercial success. Its first printing sold out before the official publication date, and it was serialized in the *Atlantic Monthly* and picked as a Book of the Month Club choice. Despite the book's occasional inaccuracies and distortions, it fixed the Stein canon once and for all, and on the strength of its success Gertrude was invited back to America for a highly successful lecture tour. It was a triumphal return. Everywhere she went she was feted as a celebrity. She was invited to tea at the White House, hostesses vied for the honor of her company, and newspapermen clustered around her like flies. One newspaper even tried weakly to parody her repetitive writing style while announcing her return home. "GERTY GERTY STEIN STEIN IS BACK HOME HOME BACK" the headline read.

Below: Alice B. Toklas and Gertrude Stein in their atelier, which contained many modern art treasures.

She had finally won. As a girl she had set out to live her life as she chose, and yet had also always sought the approval and appreciation of the fellow countrymen she had left behind. Through dogged perseverance in her own eccentricities as well as through a shrewd talent for self-advertisement, she finally succeeded in being accepted on her own terms. Few people have taken her claims to be a writer of genius seriously but she had assured herself a place in that small band of artists (to which Andy Warhol may also belong) who are remembered more for their lives and for their personalities than for their work. For a generation of Americans she personified the eccentric modernity of the Paris art world, yet to her visitors at the rue de Fleurus she seemed a familiarly American figure. There was affection as well as mockery in Scott Fitzgerald's description of her in a letter to a friend: "What an old covered-wagon she is!"

No-one would ever had called Natalie Clifford Barney anything like that. A born hedonist, she had a lightness of touch that Gertrude Stein lacked. Boredom was her only enemy, and she used every weapon that came to hand to vanquish it. She was not fundamentally a serious person. If she did not share Stein's pertinacity and capacity for work, she made up for it in her own terms with all the wit, high spirits and frivolity necessary for the successful pursuit of a life devoted to pleasure.

Above left: Stein in 1922.
Above: Romaine Brooks overdressed as a gentleman,
her preferred attire.

Natalie Barney was the daughter of a very wealthy family of mixed English, Dutch and French parentage. By an odd coincidence her salon, like Gertrude Stein's, was indirectly financed from railroad profits, as her family's fortune was based on a railroad car foundry established by her grand-father. She inherited from her father, a successful business-man in his own right, her determination and self-confidence. Her artistic inclinations came rather from her mother, who painted and who was a student and friend of Whistler.

Natalie grew up in a large house outside Cincinatti, surrounded by a small menagerie of dogs, cats, parrots, baby alligators, and a Shetland pony – the first of many horses she was to own. She first visited Europe with her parents in her early teens. While they travelled the continent, she was sent to study at the Pensionnat des Ruches, a fashionable boarding-school in Fontainebleau where her immersion in French culture, begun at home, was completed.

It was in the course of a subsequent visit to Paris with her mother that Natalie had her first significant love affair. The object of her teenage passion was Liane de Pougy, a celebrated courtesan of the Belle Epoque whom Natalie had admired while riding in the Bois de Boulogne one day. The young girl courted the older woman assiduously with flowers and letters, and was finally rewarded with the granting of a rendezvous. Dressed in a page's costume that she had bought for the occasion, she made her way to a

dimly lit boudoir in which she could barely make out a figure reclining lasciviously on a chaise-longue. The page cast herself adoringly before her master, only to discover a moment later that it was the wrong woman. Liane, who had concealed herself behind a curtain, emerged giggling with the words, "*Me voilà*."

Natalie was hastily summoned back to the family's new home in Washington, D.C., when her father discovered a letter she had received from Liane. Two years later she was back in Paris with her mother, and the career of refined Lesbianism she had started so precociously took a new turn with the start of a long and passionate friendship with the Franco-Scottish poetess Renée Vivien. This talented and beautiful young girl, though still in her teens, was already writing poems that revolved obsessively around the death wish to which she finally succumbed at the age of thirty, a victim of anorexia. Her body, already wasted by opium and alcohol, weighed just 66 pounds.

Their love affair was conducted with all the preciousness of the 1890s. The room where they met was white, furnished only with white lilies and a white bed. They fought moon-light duels with crystal swords. They travelled to the island

Below: Barney in a studious mood.
Left: A nude study of Natalie Barney.
Right: Romaine Brooks and Natalie Barney (right) had aged dramatically by 1935.
Far right: Renée Vivien, Natalie Barney's early lover.

seclusion to accompany her on excursions to the Bois de Boulogne and the Normandy countryside. He repaid the debt by making her the Amazon of his *Lettres à l'Amazone*, taking the epithet from her daily habit of riding, in a bowler hat and a black bow tie, in the Bois de Boulogne.

By the time that de Gourmont died in 1915, *l'Amazone* had established a reputation for herself in French literary circles, and particularly in that surrounding the *Mercure de France*, the review for which de Gourmont had written. She counted writers and professors among her friends, alongside the bohemian entourage with which she had surrounded herself in earlier days when the extravagant parties she threw had won her a reputation as 'the wild girl from Cincinnati'. At one gathering of her women friends, she

Above: Dolly Wilde.
Right: James Joyce, Sylvia Beach and Adrienne Monnier at Shakespeare and Co.

of Lesbos together, and dreamed of gathering a group of like-minded poetesses on Sappho's native isle. When Renée once refused to see her, Natalie, dressed in white, had herself carried to her lover's house in a coffin, with a lily on her breast. On another occasion she sought out the services of the celebrated opera singer Emma Calvé, who was also her friend. Disguised as street singers, the two made their way to Renée's window. Natalie waited her moment as Mlle. Calvé sang arias by Gluck and Puccini, and as soon as the window opened she threw in a poem attached to a bouquet of flowers. This theatrical device was less effective than it generally is on stage – it was Renée's governess who picked up the poem. All that Natalie got for her efforts was a curt note asking her not to trouble Miss Vivien further.

The affair ended tragically with Renée's death in 1909. Natalie was inconsolable. She poured out her sorrow in poems and memoirs, and then, with the instinct of a born extrovert, looked around for a fitting audience to show them to. The person she chose was a total stranger to her. Rémy de Gourmont was a distinguished writer and scholar who was then living out the last years of his life as a recluse. He had contracted lupus, a disfiguring tuberculosis of the skin, supposedly while studying medieval manuscripts in the Bibliothèque Nationale, and had given up nearly all his social contacts. He was sufficiently interested by Natalie's writings to grant her an interview in his book-filled house in the rue des Saints-Pères. Natalie's youth and wit charmed the old philosopher, and she managed to tempt him from his hired Mata Hari to appear nearly naked on a white horse harnessed with emeralds; at another, the future spy performed Javanese dances in the nude. At a Persian dinner, her guests were unexpectedly showered with rose petals dropped through a skylight by a small boy whom she had stationed earlier on the roof. She also liked to organize elaborate entertainments. At one of her soirées, Colette and the couturier Paul Poiret acted in Colette's *La Vagabonde*, while Wanda Landowska performed on the harpsichord. Colette was to become a close friend, and to live at her house for a time after the break-up of her marriage with Willy.

Natalie moved to the rue Jacob in 1909, originally to be closer to the dying Renée Vivien. She was to live there until her own death in 1972. The house she bought – number 20

in the quiet Left Bank street – dated from the seventeenth century. She furnished it with tapestries, mirrors, sofa beds covered in brown velvet, a grand piano, and photographs and portraits of herself and her friends. In the garden behind the house stood a miniature Doric temple dedicated to friendship. There was also an overgrown well, which was found, during the Second World War, to connect to an underground passageway leading to the Louvre, thus lending support to the unconfirmed rumors that the house had once belonged to Louis XIV's mistress, Ninon de Lenclos.

Throughout the twenties and thirties, Miss Barney entertained there on Friday afternoons. In comparison with her youthful escapades in Neuilly, the salon in the rue

Jacob was almost sober. One reason for this was the house itself; its floors were not considered to be strong enough to support dancing. And Natalie's tastes had also matured. Her dilettante enthusiasm for literature had grown. She had taken to expressing herself in *pensées* – though she was trilingual, speaking English, French and Italian, she normally wrote in French – and had published a volume entitled *Pensées de l'Amazone* in 1918.

By this time she moved in distinguished French literary circles. Paul Valéry visited her, as did the German poet Rilke. She was still friendly with Colette. André Gide, never given to compliments, condescended to call her one of the few people one ought to see, if one had time.

A succession of American visitors also made their way to the rue Jacob. Some, like the poet Hart Crane, were visibly impressed. Others, like William Carlos Williams, were charmed by Miss Barney herself, while expressing reservations about her salon. Some celebrities, among them Sherwood Anderson, passed in and out almost unnoticed. Natalie later, however, arranged for Anderson to address the Paris branch of the P.E.N. Club. Anderson went unwillingly, only to find – as he told Gertrude Stein later – that "it wasn't a party for me, it was a party for a big woman, and she was just a derailed freight car."

The composers George Antheil and Virgil Thomson were among her guests, and Antheil's First String Quartet was first performed at Miss Barney's on New Year's Day, 1926. Antheil was more than happy with the performance, as it netted him a commission for his Second Symphony. Sinclair Lewis visited; Natalie and he concocted plans for a magazine they would have liked to publish, to be called 'How to Live by Those who Have'. Natalie's greatest admirer among the expatriates was probably Ezra Pound. The two even co-authored a poem, which appeared under their joint signature in the *transatlantic review*.

The exact date when Natalie first met Gertrude Stein and Alice Toklas is not known, but the three of them were to remain on excellent terms for the rest of their lives. Stein noted that "Gertrude Stein and she were delighted with one another and the meeting led to many pleasant consequences," one being that she and Alice became frequent guests on Fridays at the rue Jacob. Natalie was invited to the house at Bilignin, and she reciprocated by having Gertrude and Alice to stay in the country house she shared with the portrait painter Romaine Brooks. There was an edge of mockery in Natalie's attitude towards the odd couple of the rue de Fleurus. "I am afraid 'the bigger one', who gets fatter and fatter, will sooner or later devour her," she wrote of Alice to Romaine Brooks ."She looks so thin . . ." Yet she was assiduous in her compliments about Gertrude's writings and was to write an introduction for one of her posthumously published collections.

The most distinctive feature of Miss Barney's salon continued to be the ladies with monocles and high collars, who came to declaim poems to Sappho and eye prospective conquests. The most famous of these was probably Marguerite Radclyffe Hall, 'John' to her friends. Her explicitly Lesbian novel *The Well of Loneliness* enjoyed a *succès de scandale* in the twenties and thirties, selling a million copies before the author's death in 1943. She was often to be seen in Natalie's drawing room with Una, Lady Troubridge, an Englishwoman who had left her admiral husband to live with her.

And there was Dolly Wilde who, when she first arrived in Paris in 1916, was young, beautiful and as witty as her uncle, Oscar. For the remaining 25 years of her life she was to drift from London to Paris to Italy and back, living no-one knew how. But she always remained passionately attached to Natalie, cutting her wrists on one occasion when she thought she had been jilted. Alcohol, opium and cocaine were to take their toll of her beauty, but her friendship with Natalie survived. At the time of her death from an overdose in London in 1941, they were still regular correspondents.

The Sapphic aspects of the salon at the rue Jacob did not pass without comment. Djuna Barnes, the author of *Nightwood*, produced a pseudonymous satire of it called *The Lady's Almanach*, an underground classic for many years until its author finally acknowledged and reprinted it in 1972. Radclyffe Hall features in the book as Lady Buck-and-Balk; Una, Lady Troubridge, becomes Tilly Tweed-in-Blood; while Natalie is treated rather more respectfully as Evangeline Musset. Sylvia Beach also tells the story of an ungrateful guest at the salon who, hurrying into her bookshop with a letter of introduction from Miss Barney, hissed eagerly, "Have you anything more about *those unfortunate creatures?*".

Natalie, however, had lived her life without fear of the opinions of other people. As a girl, she had found that her inheritance gave her the freedom to live as she chose, and like Gertrude Stein she had seen the world accept her non-conformism and pay hommage at her door. In the 1920s she was in the middle of her long life, an established figure in Parisian society, hostess of the most brilliant salon of her day. Paris, always tolerant of the ways of the wealthy, was her plaything. In the brittle and often cruel world of her salon, her guests were struck not only by her lavish entertaining, her wit and taste, her wardrobe by Lanvin and Schiaparelli, but even more by her self-certainty and tranquillity. In the whirlpool of opinions, discussions and flirtations, she was the still central point.

One reason for her serenity was her relationship with Romaine Brooks, the deepest and most enduring of her life. They had met in 1915. Romaine also was an heiress, beautiful and talented; for once Natalie was involved with a woman as favored by fortune as herself. Yet "the Romantic Romaine", as Somerset Maugham called her, was a profoundly unhappy woman, a classic case of the poor little rich girl born in a troubled home. Her parents' marriage had dissolved shortly after her birth. Her mother, who had inherited a substantial fortune from a multimillionaire father, spent her life travelling, abandoning her daughter for years at a stretch. Romaine's brother went mad at the age of 16. Romaine herself was to spend her life wandering through Europe like her mother, seeking but never finding a permanent home.

When she met Natalie in 1915 she was married to an English homosexual poet whom she had met on Capri. It was a nominal marriage only; the couple rarely saw each other, and the only bonds that held them together were a certain amount of mutual affection and a small cash allowance that Romaine paid him month by month. She was by 1915 a successful portraitist. Though she had held

Left: Rémy de Gourmont, by Natalie Barney.
Below: Barney's apartment in the rue Jacob.

Natalie Barney (left) and Romaine Brooks.

Below: Portrait of Natalie Barney, by Romaine Brooks.

her first exhibition only five years before, she already had two paintings in French national collections, and was later to receive the Medal of the Légion d'Honneur.

Natalie and Romaine were soon fast friends, their relationship maturing and deepening over the years into a long and watchful love affair. It was largely Natalie's presence that kept Romaine in Paris throughout the twenties and early thirties, where she lived in a ten-room studio overlooking the Seine in the sixteenth arrondissement, decorated throughout in funereal shades of black and grey. They went dancing, swimming and walking together, made excursions to Annecy and Aix-les-Bains, and when parted wrote endless sollicitous letters to each other. Romaine addressed hers to "Nat-Nat", signing them "Angel Birdie". In the thirties they bought a villa above Beauvallon with separate entrances to provide each one with the degree of privacy that she needed. They called it the *Villa Trait d'Union* – Hyphen Villa.

Despite Natalie's frequent infidelities and Romaine's recriminations, their friendship endured almost to the end of their long lives. They both lived into their nineties; when Romaine died in 1970, she was 96. It was only towards the end, when fears for her health and suspicion of other people had turned her almost into a recluse, that Romaine let the relationship falter. By that time she was living alone but for two servants in an apartment by the waterfront at Nice, with dark shades over her lamps and black coverings nailed across the windows to keep out the Mediterranean sky.

Natalie did not long survive her last love. She died two years after her, in 1972, at the age of 94. Her funeral was held on a Friday. About 50 of her friends turned up for the ceremony. It was, as her housekeeper, Mme. Berthe noted the last Friday soirée Miss Barney was to give.

However unconventional their hostesses – and unconventional hostesses were themselves something of a salon tradition – the houses of Gertrude Stein and Natalie Barney had both performed the traditional functions of literary salons, as places where writers met and ideas were exchanged. There was one other American establishment in Paris that, while not properly a salon, played something of the same role. Shakespeare and Company, the English-language bookstore founded and run by Sylvia Beach, was more than just a place to buy books. It also served as an information bureau, a meeting-place and even a forwarding address for American writers in Paris, many of whom – including Ernest Hemingway – were almost daily visitors there.

Its proprietor – Hemingway called her Madame Shakespeare – was a minister's daughter from New Jersey, where Woodrow Wilson and his family had been members of her father's congregation. She first came to Paris at the age of 14 when her father took charge of the Students' *Atelier Réunions*, a series of weekly musical soirées for American students. The family later returned to America, but Sylvia had developed an interest in France, and particularly French literature, that proved strong enough to take her back to the city in 1917, when German troops were barely fifty miles away and bombs and shells were exploding daily in the streets.

It was at this unpropitious time that she met a French-woman who was to affect the entire future course of her life. Adrienne Monnier was the friendly, buxom and energetic owner of a bookstore in the rue de l'Odéon that she had opened two years previously. In the full-skirted *paysanne-de-Paris* costume she always wore, she was a striking Latin Quarter figure, looking as though she had just emerged, in costume, from a character performance at the Odéon Théâtre down the street. She shared with Sylvia Beach an almost religious devotion for books and their authors, and she was already friendly with a distinguished circle of French writers that included Paul Valéry, Léon-Paul Fargue, Jean Cocteau and André Gide. Each of the two women was curious about the other's native literature, and they were soon close friends. The friendship was to provide Sylvia with a vocation and a home; it was at Adrienne Monnier's instigation that Shakespeare and Company was founded, and the two were to live together in a flat down the road for sixteen years.

The original Shakespeare and Company was opened in 1919, in a disused laundry in the rue Dupuytren. Two years later, the shop moved around the corner to larger and more frequented premises at 12 rue de l'Odéon, opposite Adrienne Monnier's shop. It was to remain there for the next twenty years.

The rue de l'Odéon bookstore was a warm, comfortable place, with a big stove and with photographs of contemporary writers on the walls. Its owner encouraged her friends to visit her, making the shop an informal forum for the literary gossip of the day. She also acted as a go-between for resident writers and Americans who had just arrived in town. Sherwood Anderson went to see her before first contacting Gertrude Stein, a regular customer who had also been the first subscriber to the lending library Sylvia Beach ran from the shop. Sylvia sent a note to the rue de Fleurus, stressing Anderson's admiration for Gertrude Stein's writing. Miss Stein wrote back immediately, inviting Anderson to visit her. It was the start of a lifelong friendship.

The international fame of Shakespeare and Company was built largely on the strength of its one and only publishing venture. Sylvia had long admired the writings of James Joyce. She first met the man himself only three days after his arrival in Paris in 1920, and he was soon a regular visitor to the shop in the rue Dupuytren. It was there that he complained one day of his despair of finding anyone to bring out *Ulysses*; the editors of the *Little Review* in New York had been found guilty of obscenity for publishing extracts from it, and the book had also encountered legal difficulties in England. Sylvia Beach at once enquired if Shakespeare and Company could have the honor of publishing it, and Joyce eagerly accepted the offer. So it was that Miss Beach, the clergyman's daughter, served as midwife for the birth of the most famous banned book of her day.

The first copy of the blue-and-white volume that was to make her shop world famous was ready in time for Joyce's 40th birthday on February 2, 1922. Even before its appearance the book had built up a huge underground reputation on the strength of the excerpts the reviews had printed and from its unsought courtroom publicity. Throughout the twenties, buying a *Ulysses* from Shakespeare and Company was to be an essential part of any literary-minded visitor's trip to Paris. Even George Gershwin called in for a copy. The shop itself became something of a tourist attraction. At one time American Express coaches used to stop briefly outside it on guided tours of the city.

Sylvia Beach remained friendly with Joyce, even though she found him a difficult man with whom to work. He added almost 90,000 words – the size of a good-length novel – to his original manuscript on proof, driving the book's French typesetters to distraction and almost forcing his publisher into liquidation. Joyce, however, took her services very much for granted. When *Ulysses* was finally cleared of obscenity charges by the District Court of New York in 1933 clearing the way for an American edition, he expected her to waive all claims to the book, and set about negotiating with other publishers without consulting her. He eventually made a deal with Random House that guaranteed him a forty-five thousand dollar advance; Sylvia Beach received not a single cent. He did at one time have the grace to thank her for her work with a verse tribute, parodying Shakespeare's *Who is Sylvia?*

. . . Then to Sylvia let us sing
Her daring lies in selling.
She can sell each mortal thing
That's boring beyond telling
To her let us buyers bring.

Throughout her career she was to retain her deep admiration for authors, whose interests she served with a disinterested devotion. Occasionally she was over-protective. She irritated the Canadian writer Morley Callaghan, who had come to Paris largely at Hemingway's instigation, by refusing to give him the current address of his old friend. Once when George Moore and Joyce were both in her shop at the same time, she failed to introduce them, despite the inquisitive glances they cast at each other and at her. She had not wanted to risk offending or embarrassing either one. As a result of her caution, the two never met.

Writers generally appreciated her efforts on their behalf. Through her tact and shrewdness she managed to retain the affection even of such difficult customers as Hemingway, who once punched the heads off three dozen tulips decorating her shop after reading an attack on his writing. Her bookstore remained one of his fondest memories of his early days in Paris, and he was to write of her in *A Moveable Feast* that "no-one that I ever knew was nicer to me".

The most touching proof of the gratitude that writers felt for her was to come in the difficult days of the 1930s. With her French customers buying fewer books and the number of American visitors reduced to a trickle, she found herself in serious financial difficulties and was considering closing up shop. André Gide, an old friend, found out about her difficulties. After an unsuccessful attempt to get cash support from the French government, he set about organizing a body called the Friends of Shakespeare and Company

Above: Sylvia Beach in her famous bookshop in the rue de l'Odéon.
Left: Beach and Ernest Hemingway in front of Shakespeare and Company.

to help save the shop. Its committee included such eminent French writers as Paul Valéry, Georges Duhamel, André Maurois, Jules Romains and Jean Paulhan. Several writers gave public readings as well as money to help her. Her English and American friends also rallied to the cause. Hemingway and Stephen Spender, fresh from the Spanish Civil War, gave a joint reading. T. S. Eliot even flew over from London. As a result of their efforts, the shop was able to stay in business until 1941, when the German occupation authorities, less conscious of Sylvia's services to literature than of her status as an enemy alien, finally forced Shakespeare and Company to close down.

4. The Lost Generation

There are several versions of the story that gave the Lost Generation its name, but the most plausible seems to be this. One summer in Belley, Gertrude Stein's Ford car needed some attention, and it was serviced quickly and thoroughly by a young garage mechanic at the hotel where she was staying. She mentioned the young man's efficiency to the proprietor, her friend M. Pernollet. Yes, he replied, boys of his age made good workers. It was different with the ones who had gone to the war. Young men became civilized between the ages of 18 and 25, and the soldiers had missed that civilizing experience. They were, he said, *une génération perdue*.

Hemingway heard the story at the rue de Fleurus. When he was working on his first novel it came back to him, for he was writing about the 'uncivilized', aimless lives of the very people M. Pernollet had in mind. He used the sentence "You are all a lost generation" (attributed to Gertrude Stein) as an epigraph for the book, thereby guaranteeing it enduring fame.

In its original sense, the description only applied to survivors of the war who, like the characters in *The Sun Also Rises*, had been unable or unwilling to settle back into the routines of peacetime life. But, in the way of catch phrases, the words were used by other writers more and more loosely, until 'The Lost Generation' came to convey the whole anonymous horde of young Americans abroad, particularly those with literary or artistic inclinations.

Paris was indisputably the capital city of the Lost Generation. It passed, of course, through other towns en route, from Munich to Madrid, Pamplona to Rapallo. Humphrey Bogart's Casablanca can even be counted as a border outpost. But the greatest concentration of expatriates was always to be found in Paris, and more specifically in the streets around the boulevard Montparnasse that provided the scene for the first part of Hemingway's novel. It was there that the wanderers came closest to finding a home.

The city had a double attraction for writers. Its artistic reputation had never been higher. It was the home of all that was most daringly modern. As Gertrude Stein used to say, Paris was where the twentieth century was. Secondly, it was also a city where Americans could live well on very little money. Even young writers with nothing to show for their ambitions but bundles of rejection slips could live like boulevardiers on small allowances from back home. In the exchange bonanza of the 1920s it took real dedication to starve. Writers who had always wanted to live in Paris suddenly made the discovery that it was a practical economic proposition.

Ezra Pound was one of the first to arrive coming from England where he had lived throughout the war. He had come to the conclusion that postwar London was dead. "There is no longer any intellectual *life* in England," he wrote to William Carlos Williams in 1920, "save what centers in this eight by ten pentagonal room." He and his wife Dorothy moved to what he called "the Island of Paris" convinced that it was the one live spot in Europe and hoping to find there "a poetic serum to save English letters from postmature and American letters from premature suicide and decomposition."

He soon made his presence felt on the Paris literary scene, at the salons in the rue Jacob and the rue de Fleurus and in the little magazines. He was living in a ground floor flat in the rue Notre-Dame-des-Champs, where he set about making the furniture he needed from packing-cases, canvas and wooden boards. Though reticent about his writing, he was boastful on the subject of his carpentry. He used to point out the fine points of the workmanship to guests who came to perch uncomfortably on the hard wooden chairs.

Soon writers were arriving thick and fast. Sherwood Anderson paid his first brief visit in 1921. Later that year the 22-year-old Ernest Hemingway arrived in town with his bride, Hadley. He was a shy, good looking young man, who tended to listen more than talk. He was living off his wife's allowance and the income from occasional pieces written for a Canadian newspaper.

Left: Closing time at the Café aux Deux Magots.
Below: 'La Bolée' strikes a grandiloquent pose.

Above: The *Lapin Agile* derived its name from its owner, Gill, who saw himself as a 'nimble rabbit'.

One newcomer who made an immediate impression in the cafés was Robert McAlmon. People were struck by his laconic good looks and his distinctive nasal drawl. While earning his living as an artist's model in New York, he had met a young English writer who called herself Bryher. She happened to be the daughter of Sir John Ellerman a shipping magnate who was then one of the wealthiest men in Britain. Bryher who was looking for a way of escaping from her family's surveillance suggested a marriage of convenience to McAlmon. In return for the comparative freedom she would gain as a married woman, she offered the chance to live in Paris and a part of her allowance. McAlmon agreed. They escaped as soon as possible from the oppressive family mansion in London to the Left Bank, where he and his wife were free to go their own ways.

Another significant visitor in the summer of 1921 was Scott Fitzgerald. Unlike Hemingway and McAlmon, Fitzgerald had already made a name for himself with his first novel. Zelda and he spent only a few days in Paris at this time. Three disillusioning years were to pass before the two of them, worn out with parties, were to return to the city where Scott had decided that they could work, live cheaply and escape from the burden of their friends.

Throughout the twenties, when money was plentiful and exchange rates favorable, other writers drifted in and out of town. Some, like the critic Malcolm Cowley and the Southern poet Allen Tate, came on fellowships to study at French universities. William Carlos Williams took a sabbatical from medical practice to taste Parisian literary life and to look up old friends. The mercurial John Dos Passos made fleeting visits on journeys that were to take him

through much of Europe, North Africa and the Middle East. He stayed long enough to become friendly with Hemingway, and to go to the fiesta in Pamplona with "a lot of fake bohemians" – his view of the future cast of *The Sun Also Rises*. Ford Madox Ford, novelist and future editor of the *transatlantic review*, came to Paris from England, and Ezra Pound persuaded James Joyce to move up from Trieste. Marriage to a Frenchman brought the novelist Kay Boyle over from Cincinatti. At least one writer – the tubercular Irish-American poet Ernest Walsh – came to France to die.

Not the least of Paris's attractions for writers was that it was a good place to get published. It was the home of a succession of expatriate literary reviews. The first of these was Ford Madox Ford's *transatlantic review*, edited from a loft on the Ile St. Louis. Ford, with his shambling manner and the wheezing voice that had led Norman Douglas to call him an 'animated adenoid' was something of a figure of fun for the Americans, but he was a good editor who published Pound, Hemingway and Stein among others. When the *transatlantic* sank for want of money, the gap it left was filled by Ernest Walsh's *This Quarter*. In the late twenties the baton passed to Eugene Jolas' *transition*, the most enduring of them all; it survived almost until the Second World War.

In addition to the reviews there were a number of adventurous, small scale publishers willing to handle serious new work. A newspaperman called William Bird printed the publications of the Three Mountains Press (which included work by Pound and Hemingway) on his own hand-press. This was so big, and the offices that housed it so small, that Bird had to go out into the street to talk to visitors. Another outlet for American writing was Harry Crosby's Black Sun Press, which was to publish Hart Crane. The output of most of these organizations was small, yet it can rarely have been easier for expatriate writers to get their work into print.

The literary colony was based in Montparnasse, known familiarly as the Quarter. In the center of Montparnasse, then as now, lay the four large cafés that dominate the crossroads where the boulevard Montparnasse meets the boulevard Raspail. The Coupole and the Rotonde, the Dôme and the Sélect soon had international reputations. By 1925 critics of the older generation were using phrases like 'the school of the Rotonde' to describe, usually disparagingly, a new undercurrent in American literature. The twenties' expatriates were as closely identified with these cafés as Sartre and the Existentialists were with the Flore and the Deux Magots in the boulevard Saint Germain in their day.

In his book *That Summer in Paris*, the Canadian novelist Morley Callaghan gives a description of a typical day in Montparnasse at that time. His wife and he would get up around noon and stroll to the Coupole for lunch. In the afternoon they would make their way to the American Express office on the Right Bank to check for mail before returning to their flat, where Callaghan would put in a couple of hours of writing. By six o'clock they were back in the Coupole for an aperitif. After dinner they would move to the Sélect, where they would spend the rest of the evening talking and drinking.

The cafés were the stages on which the daily comedy of Montparnasse's literary life was played out, and their proprietors were important behind-the-scenes characters in it. Gaston, barman and part owner of the Coupole, was popular for his discretion and his quiet generosity towards artists. The patron at the Rotonde, on the other hand, was little loved. Having bought what had, under the previous owner Libion, been an artists' café patronized by Modigliani and Kisling, he set about smartening it up. Waiters were no longer given instructions not to wake customers who fell asleep at the tables. Instead, wealthy bourgeois patrons brought their wives and mistresses to dine in the grill-room the new owner had installed. Business prospered, but old habitués of the Quarter were outraged.

They were also uncertain about the Sélect. The *patronne* there was known simply as Mme. Sélect and it was said of her that her evenings were not complete without a good argument. She met her match in the poet Hart Crane. One night he went on a whiskey binge, and the pile of saucers on his table had mounted high before a waiter asked him to settle the bill. Crane confessed that he had only fifty centimes on him. Mme. Sélect intervened, and the argument grew heated. There were plenty of Americans in the café at the time who would gladly have paid the money due, but by that time Crane was fighting drunk and looking for trouble. He began by insulting Mme. Sélect, then broadened his field of attack to the entire French nation. The *patronne* called for the police. In the interval before they arrived, Crane floored four waiters who were trying to restrain him. Finally a solitary *flic* appeared, and to the ill-concealed delight of the café's other customers, Crane felled him with one blow. Reinforcements came, and after a last-ditch resistance involving tables and bottles the poet was overcome. He was finally dragged from the café by his feet.

Above: Dolly's Bar was named after one of the Dolly Sisters of American vaudeville who founded it.

Above: The F. Scott Fitzgeralds on the beach at Antibes.

Above: F. Scott Fitzgerald, Scottie (their daughter) and Zelda in their golden twenties.

Above: The Fitzgeralds took a stateroom on their way to Paris in 1925.

Crane was not the only American poet to get into trouble with the Paris police. E. E. Cummings, who had returned to live in France despite his experiences of internment there, was again to see the inside of a French prison. After an evening spent drinking with Dos Passos and the critic Gilbert Seldes at the Café de la Paix, he stopped on his way home in a dark little Latin Quarter street, the rue Gît-le-Coeur, to relieve himself. At that moment a gendarme appeared and arrested him. He was taken to the police station, his friends Dos Passos and Seldes following him. Seldes claimed to have heard this dialogue between the gendarme who made the arrest and the officer on desk-duty:
"*Un Américain qui pisse.*"
"*Quoi? Encore un pisseur américain?*"
Despite the ludicrous aspects of the situation, Cummings and his friends were nervous as a result of the poet's wartime internment. To save him from having to appear in a magistrate's court, representations were made to the French writer Paul Morand, who held an influential post in the French Foreign Office. By a couple of discreet telephone calls, Morand was able to ensure that Cummings was released that night. He returned to his friends' flat to be greeted by hastily prepared posters demanding "REPRIEVE PISSEUR AMERICAIN".

Earlier, Crane had written to a friend, "Paris really is a test for an American." Working was the test, and amid the distractions of Montparnasse's night life many would-be writers failed it. The temptations were many and varied, and what Pound called "the island of Paris" could make a lotus-eater of any young writer whose dedication faltered. T. S. Eliot was very aware of this. It was one of the reasons why he, alone of the twenties' literary exiles, chose London as his home. "If I came to live in Paris", he wrote to Robert McAlmon, "the first thing to do would be to cut myself off from it, and not depend upon it."

Cutting oneself off from the life of the Quarter was not easy though. Without some degree of self-discipline a writer's days and nights soon became too short for writing. Hemingway was maybe more aware of this than anyone. He would get up early in the morning to start writing before the streets were noisy enough to be a distraction. He hired a garret room in the hotel in the rue du Cardinal Lemoine where the poet Verlaine had died, in which he could work alone and in peace. Later he took to writing in cafés in the daytime when there were few people to disturb him. Looking back on those days near the end of his life, he was to write: "The blue-backed notebooks, the two pencils and the pencil-sharpener (a pocket-knife was too wasteful), the marble-topped tables, the smell of early morning, sweeping out and mopping and luck were all you needed."

Perhaps luck was just another word for dedication. Whatever it was, other talents of the Quarter did not have it. Robert McAlmon was to be the prime literary casualty of Paris in the twenties. At the time of his arrival, his wit, charm and intelligence had seemed to guarantee him success. He was a generous patron of other people's talents. He published Hemingway's first book, as well as work by Stein, Ford and William Carlos Williams. But his own writing languished. Occasionally little magazines published poems or short stories of his, and he put together a couple of thin collections of his work neither of which received much attention. He spent more and more of his time in cafés and night clubs, where, one observer noted, "the drinks were always on him, and alas! often in him." Café wits re-christened him McAlimony, and an unkind little poem appeared in *transition*:
I'd rather live in Oregon
And pack salmon
Than live in Nice
And write like Robert McAlmon.
He quarreled with many of his old friends, among them

Above: The famous café La Rotonde in Montparnasse.

Hemingway. Joyce was the only writer he managed not to offend, and that was only by dint of a curious strategem. Whenever he found himself getting drunk in Joyce's presence, he would excuse himself, go to the bathroom, and force himself to vomit. Then he would wash his face, straighten his hair and clothes, and reappear at the dinner table perfectly sober.

If McAlmon's career was a disappointment, Scott Fitzgerald's came closer to tragedy. He returned to Paris in 1924. His life style was, from the start, different from that of the other expatriates. Because of the success of his first novels, he had a great deal more money than they did, and he chose to live on the Right Bank, in an expensive, gloomy flat near the Arc de Triomphe. He divided his time in France between Paris and the Riviera. To begin with, he worked. He finished *The Great Gatsby*, and it was immediately successful, at least with the critics. In many ways he was at the peak of his career. Yet Hemingway, who

Below: A busy afternoon at La Rotonde.

met him at this time, quickly noticed his unreliability and his inability to hold drink.

In the years that followed he worked less and drank more. Zelda and he spent much time and money in the Montmartre cabarets. One such night, Zelda gave a pearl necklace that Scott had just bought for her to a black girl she had been dancing with. That time they were lucky – the girl gave it back the next morning. Other beneficiaries of the Fitzgerald largesse had fewer scruples.

Scott had developed a habit of waking up his friends at all hours of the night, usually to share a bottle of champagne with them. Evenings regularly ended with the same friends helping him into a taxi to carry him home. Sometimes they had to dissuade him from giving the driver the entire contents of his wallet to pay the fare. Things got worse when the Fitzgeralds returned to Paris in 1928, after a year in America. By the end of the decade the golden couple of the Flapper Era were spinning down twin vortexes of alcohol and madness. Zelda was soon after institutionalized, and Scott made his way to Hollywood.

Drinking was an important part of the life style of the Quarter. Whether in reaction to Prohibition or as a natural side-effect of café life, the writers took to alcohol with gusto. Some, like Hart Crane with his Cutty Sark whiskey, were one-drink men, but the majority were more catholic in their tastes. "They drank cocktails before meals like Americans, wines and brandies like Frenchmen, beer like Germans, whiskey-and-soda like the English," wrote Fitzgerald. Ezra Pound disapproved; this was one of the reasons that finally led him to quit Paris for Italy.

Drugs were not then the regular part of bohemian literary life they were one day to become. In Berlin at the time a deck of cocaine could be bought for the equivalent of ten cents; but in Paris only hard-core bohemians and poets who had plunged into romantic decadence took dope. One was Ralph Cheever Dunning. Ezra Pound, who admired his

poetry and took an interest in his well-being, kept a supply of raw brown opium in a cold cream jar to give to him in emergencies. When Pound left Paris, the task was passed to Hemingway. The only time he was called upon to deliver it – by Dunning's distraught concierge – the poet took the jar, looked in it, and then threw it at him with considerable force, together with a follow-up volley of empty milk bottles. Hemingway never discovered what he had done to offend him.

In sexual matters the mood of the Quarter was one of tolerance. Gertrude Stein's relationship with Alice Toklas was rarely commented on, and Robert McAlmon could boast in the cafés of his bisexuality without arousing much concern. Natalie Barney's salon was explicitly Sapphic. Writers with a taste for inversion could also explore less renfined haunts like the Gipsy Bar on the boulevard Edgar Quinet where the notorious Dr. Maloney, self-proclaimed abortionist, professional boxer, homosexual célèbre, irrepressible backwoodsman and original Irish tenor, held court to an audience of Lesbians and ageing transvestites.

Those of more conventional taste contented themselves with the company of the chorus girls, demi-mondaines, and artists' models who crowded the café terraces. The most famous of these were Kiki, best known of the Montparnasse models, and an American girl from the Folies called Florence Martin. One of the favorite stories of the Quarter concerned a couple of visiting American ladies who were touring Montparnasse in search of night life. As their taxi drew up outside the Dingo Bar, Florence Martin emerged shouting a string of obscenities. First lady to second lady, enthusiastically: "*This* must be the place."

No writer, however strong his liver and his appetite for life, could have survived for long on undiluted doses of Montparnasse night life, and many of them took up sports to restore their health. One of the few things that Pound and

Hemingway in Paris had in common with T. S. Eliot in London at this time was that they all boxed. Hemingway was particularly dedicated, and several of his friends were astonished, on visiting him, to be presented with gloves and made to defend themselves. Later, sparring with friends in the gym at the American Club became a regular part of his Paris life. Morley Callaghan was one of his most frequent partners. The painter Miro once acted as timekeeper for them.

Another time Scott Fitzgerald volunteered for this job, and what followed was to mark an important step in the cooling of his friendship with Hemingway. Callaghan, who was smaller than Hemingway but had had the advantage of having trained with good college boxers in Toronto, knocked him down. Fitzgerald, who had been absorbed in the fight, then realized that he had let the round run a minute too long. As he began to apologize, Hemingway cut him off: "All right, Scott, If you want to see me getting the shit knocked out of me, just say so. Only don't say you made a mistake." He then strode off to the showers, leaving Fitzgerald pale with shock. It was a remark dropped in the heat of the moment, and nothing more was said about it; but neither had ever spoken to the other in that tone before, and neither was to forget it.

Hemingway also liked to watch boxing matches. He used to go to the fights at the Cirque de Paris, and he once took Sylvia Beach who had no known interest in the sport to see a bout in Ménilmontant. The bookshop owner enjoyed it immensely, less for the fight itself than for Hemingway's running commentary. She was rewarded with a visit to Hemingway's subsequent discovery, the bicycle races at the Vélodrome d'Hiver.

Earlier Hemingway had gone through a horse racing phase and had spent a lot of time and money at Enghien and Auteuil. He was not the only writer with a taste for the turf.

Left: Le Dôme in September 1929.
Below: An advertising leaflet for La Coupole.
Bottom: Sketch of Le Dôme. Le Dôme and La Coupole were popular meeting places for writers and artists.
Right: La Coupole in 1934.

Restaurant
Bar américain

Dancing
Thé dansant

LA COUPOLE

Service

permanent

LA COUPOLE
102, B^rd du Montparnasse - Danton 68-64 et 65

Harold Stearns was another. This interesting individual had made a reputation for himself in America after the war as an editor and writer. In 1921 he took the boat for Paris where he became the most dedicated of the Quarter's barflies, served as the model for Harvey Stone in *The Sun Also Rises*, and earned a precarious living as a racing tipster for the *Chicago Tribune*'s Paris edition. His shabby, unshaven figure was pointed out to newcomers as a warning of the dangers of the Quarter. Stearns was inventive in his search for drinking money. He would talk movingly of a steeplechaser that had broken its leg taking a jump at one of the local courses. He had persuaded the racecourse authorities not to destroy the horse, but had only been able to save it by taking the responsibility for its welfare. But the horse was expensive to keep, and he could no longer afford the vet's bills. It was a touching story, and few of the visitors he told it to could hear it without wanting to help. Stearns would circle the terrace tables, telling his tale; then he would make his way back to the bar, a sad smile on his face and his pockets jingling.

Ezra Pound who was occasionally one of Hemingway's sparring partners, found that music was his most serious distraction. Despite relative poverty, he bought himself a bassoon and his playing quickly became one of the jokes of the Quarter. John Rodker, one of his publishers, used to say that the sounds that came out of it were so strange that it was difficult to gauge how far they fell short of what was expected of them. Pound was not easily discouraged, and soon developed an ambition to write an opera, both words and music. Selections from his *Testament*, based on the life of François Villon, were in fact performed at the Salle Pleyel in June 1925, before a packed house. T. S. Eliot even came over from London. The opera was unexpectedly successful, and was subsequently broadcast in its entirety in Britain by the B.B.C.

Above: The novelist Kay Boyle.

The pace of Parisian life was hectic, and a time came when every writer needed to escape from the city. The train and car trips they made through a Europe in which travelling was easier than it ever had been before did much to give their work the cosmopolitan flavor that is one of its attractions. The Fitzgeralds gravitated naturally to the Mediterranean – St. Raphael, Juan-les-Pins, Antibes. "One could get away with more on the summer Riviera," Scott wrote later, "and whatever happened seemed to have something to do with art." Hemingway liked the mountains of Switzerland and Austria, the Basque trout streams, and of course the bull rings of Spain, which Gertrude Stein had initially advised him to visit. Hart Crane spent several months in Collioure, a fishing village near the Spanish border, that Matisse and the Fauvists had earlier frequented.

Walking tours were popular. Dos Passos, on one of his whirlwind visits to France, joined Robert McAlmon and others of the bull-fighting crowd from Pamplona for a gruelling thirteen-day trek through the Spanish Pyrenees to Andorra. Even T. S. Eliot put on a rucksack for a few days of hiking with Ezra Pound around Excideuil in Provence.

One strange side-effect of all the travelling was to increase the writers' sense of their own nationality. The more new lands they explored, the more American they felt themselves to be. All of them, with the exception of the long-time exiles like Ezra Pound and Gertrude Stein, finally made the decision to go back to America. For a few, like Thomas Wolfe, who on all of his visits to France was dejectedly

homesick, the desire to get back was immediate and urgent. For most of them it was slow-maturing, and it took the incentive provided by the Depression to send them home. It wasn't so much a question of disillusionment with Europe – though they found out soon enough that the grass there wasn't always as green as they had imagined at the start. It was more a realization that in the long run it wasn't the place where they belonged.

Perhaps because of this, they tended to keep their own company. Few of them had close French friends. Their relations with French writers were cordial but distant. Blaise Cendrars was an amusing dinner companion. Most of them knew Cocteau's poetry, if not the poet himself. Yet when William Carlos Williams, visiting Paris, asked his old friend Robert McAlmon to introduce him to the younger French writers, McAlmon was nonplussed. Although he was at the heart of American literary activity in the Quarter, he hardly knew a single French writer of his own generation.

One pleasant result of their sense of isolation was the spirit of mutual aid that existed in the Quarter. If an artist of any kind was in trouble, steps would be taken to help him out. In this kind of situation, Ezra Pound was the most disinterestedly generous of them all. It was he who instigated the wild scheme to rescue T. S. Eliot from the drudgery of his job in a London bank, a plan that Natalie Barney christened 'Bel Esprit'. Pound's idea was to find thirty donors willing to guarantee Eliot £10 a year each for as long as the poet should need it. It had many drawbacks, not the least being that Eliot himself was disinclined to throw himself onto other people's charity. When he started receiving anonymous gifts in the post – on one occasion someone sent him four postage stamps – his pride was roused, and he eventually ordered Pound to put an end to the fund raising. Pound was equally concerned for Joyce's welfare, and the author of *Ulysses* was once surprised to receive a large brown parcel from him in which he had solicitously enclosed some old clothes and a pair of worn brown shoes.

The distribution of Joyce's banned novel in the United States was a more serious affair. Here Hemingway was the one to help. He put Sylvia Beach in touch with a friend of his who was moving to Canada, where no such ban existed. This anonymous friend was sent copies for all the native Americans who had subscribed before the New York customs officials had begun to intercept deliveries. With the aid of one accomplice, he smuggled the big blue-and-white volumes one by one by ferry across the border. The greatest novel of the century entered the United States in the seat of someone's pants.

Someone was usually found to help an artist with money troubles. When Ernest Walsh improvidently booked himself into a suite at Claridge's and found that he had no money to pay the bill, a wealthy lady writer came forward to settle it for him. At one time a rumor spread that the American composer George Antheil needed treatment for tuberculosis. A fund was at once organized to pay for it, and Antheil gratefully accepted the proceeds. No more was ever heard of the tuberculosis or of the money.

The only occasion on which mutual aid failed was the sad case of the Japanese artist Toda. He was a familiar face around the cafés, and his work was generally admired, but

Above: A 'masculine' interchange at Le Monocle, a popular lesbian night club.
Below: The crowded bar at La Rotonde.

little was known of his private life or circumstances. Then one day he was found dead in his hotel room. He had starved to death rather than suffer the indignity of letting people know that he needed money.

There was much generosity in the Quarter, but there was also an abnormal amount of back-biting. The atmosphere was competitive, and literary success was forgiven with difficulty. When Sinclair Lewis arrived in Paris flushed with the triumph of *Main Street*, he was not well received. He made the mistake of boasting about the number of copies his books had sold. One evening at the Dôme, as he drunkenly compared his writing to Flaubert's, a voice from a neighboring table cruelly cut the future Nobel Prizewinner short. "Sit down. You're just a best-seller."

Writers friendships also tended to crack and split under the pressure of success. The gulf between Hemingway and Fitzgerald had widened, and a stupid malentendu was to come between the two and their friend and joint protégé, Morley Callaghan. An inaccurate report of his bout with Hemingway appeared in the gossip column of a New York newspaper. According to it, Callaghan had knocked out Hemingway in one round. This touched Hemingway on a raw nerve, and he cajoled Fitzgerald into sending a telegram collect to Callaghan in Toronto to demand a correction. Callaghan, who had already written to the newspaper to

Above left: Ernest Walsh.
Above right: Janet Flanner, 'Genet', whose 'Letter from Paris' fascinated readers of *The New Yorker*.

Above: La Marquise Casati at the Beaumont Ball 1927.
Left: Hemingway when he wrote *The Sun Also Rises*.

explain the columnist's mistake, was understandably angry. As the mutual misunderstandings became apparent, feelings cooled down. Even so, Callaghan was never to see either of the other two again.

By that time it was 1930, and the Quarter was breaking up. In one sense it collapsed under the weight of its own reputation. From 1924 onwards, a growing number of articles had been appearing in American newspapers and magazines about the dissolute, wasteful and immensely attractive lives of the writers and artists who lived in it. The triumph of *The Sun Also Rises* put the finishing touches to this unintentional publicity campaign. By the late twenties it seemed as though no college student's education was complete without a spell of hard drinking in the Montparnasse cafés. Other tourists took up the scent, and soon the writers no longer felt at home in the district whose image they had done so much to propagate. "Paris was by now completely finished, with all of the old crowd gone and the Quarter impossible," Robert McAlmon wrote in 1930, before setting off for Mexico.

The Crash came as a kind of *coup de grâce*. Until that time, money had never been a major problem. Jobs had unexpectedly materialized whenever writers needed them. Kay Boyle and the Canadian poet John Glassco had both lived in luxury for a time ghost-writing the memoirs of the Dayang Muda – the English ex-wife of a member of the

Sarawak royal family. They had moved into her expensive apartment, where they amused themselves between meals by inventing extravagant anecdotes about celebrities the old lady claimed to have known in her youth. Glassco had also at one time put his youthful good looks to use by performing in pornographic films and making assignations with wealthy Frenchwomen in a *maison de rendezvous*. But by 1930 casual work, whether licit or illicit, was getting hard to find. More importantly, the checks from back home were getting fewer and smaller. Paris remained an attractive place to visit, but it was no longer so easy to live there.

These were the years of the long journey home. McAlmon made his way to Mexico; he was later to wind up working for his brother in El Paso, Texas. Hemingway gave up Paris for Key West and Spain, where he was gathering material in the summers for *Death in the Afternoon*. Scott Fitzgerald stayed on into 1931, but only to remain in touch with Zelda, by then a patient in a psychiatric hospital in Switzerland, where for the first time she had been diagnosed as a schizophrenic. Pound had long since settled in Rapallo. Even Harold Stearns went back to America to resume the career he had abandoned as a writer and critic. By the mid-thirties, Gertrude Stein and Sylvia Beach were the literary colony's only long term, surviving inhabitants.

Other writers continued to visit Paris throughout the 1930s, but only one important new talent went there to live. That was Henry Miller, and the Paris he described in *Tropic of Cancer* was a different city from the place the writers of the twenties had known. Hart Crane, who barely outlived the decade, had described that other city at its most extravagant on a postcard to a friend: "Dinners, soirées, poets, erratic millionaires, painters, translations, lobsters, absinthe, music, promenades, oysters, sherry, aspirins, pictures, Sapphic heiresses, editors, books, sailors. *And how!*" In retrospect it has the unreal glamor of a party from a Scott Fitzgerald novel, but by the early thirties the party was over and the guests had all gone home.

5. Avant-Garde

The writers of the Lost Generation went to France to think about America. Paris was for them merely a background against which the drama of their own lives and their largely American concerns was played out. There were, however, other Americans for whom the city played a more positive role. They were those who were attracted by its reputation as a metropolis of the arts and, above all, as the center of the contemporary avant-garde. Most of them were painters, sculptors, composers, musicians – artists whose work was not affected by the French language barrier. Yet there were a couple of writers who were drawn, for a time at least, into the maelstrom of literary and anti-literary activity that agitated French cultural life immediately after the war.

In 1919 the front-runners of the Parisian avant-garde were the Dadaists. The prewar art movements, Fauvism and Cubism, had lost much of their impetus, and although individual artists continued to produce valuable work in their styles, they were no longer attracting neophytes. Dada, however, was a child of the war. It encompassed all the arts in one grand, nihilistic gesture. It had taken the joyful absurdities of earlier poets like Alfred Jarry and Guillaume Apollinaire and, in the midst of a world bent on self-destruction, had given them a bitter twist. Even its name was meaningless; *dada*, a child's word for 'horse', was chosen at random from the dictionary. Dada's aim was to negate and to shock, and the artists associated with it set about their mission with savage glee.

Dada had been born in the cafés and cabarets of wartime Switzerland, but with the Armistice its leader, the Rumanian Tristan Tzara, moved to Paris. He and his supporters spread the Dada message through manifestos, magazines and public meetings in which literature and art were derided and the audience insulted. They staged a public trial of the distinguished writer and nationalist Maurice Barrès, accusing him of "high crimes against the security of the human spirit". The poet Benjamin Péret gave evidence for the prosecution dressed in a gas mask and a tattered German Army uniform as 'the Unknown Soldier'; shouting "Long live France and fried potatoes", he launched into such a vitriolic denunciation of Barrès and of patriotism in general that his comrades had eventually to rescue him from the hands of the enraged audience.

After Dada metamorphosed into Surrealism in 1923, the spirit of outrage remained as strong as ever. The Surrealists celebrated the state funeral of the writer Anatole France by dancing in the wake of the cortege and by handing out a tract entitled *A Cadaver*, one of whose sections was headed "Have you ever slapped a corpse?".

Left: Two ladies of the world entertain a would-be artist of the *demi-monde* on champagne at the Coupole in Montparnasse in 1926.

The two American writers who came into closest contact with Dadaism were Matthew Josephson and Malcolm Cowley. Both were later to be dignified by respectable academic reputations in America, Josephson as a biographer, Cowley as a critic, leaving Dadaism far behind them. Their Dadaist phase was little more than a sowing of literary wild oats, yet at the time the movement had a decisive influence on them.

Josephson was the first of the two to get in touch with the group, on his arrival in Paris in 1921. At the time he was scraping a living by writing occasional articles for American magazines, though he later got a regular job on an English-language racing-sheet called the *Paris Telegram*.

Josephson came close enough to the group to join them in their almost daily meetings which were generally conducted in a dingy café in the Passage de l'Opéra (now destroyed). They were conspiratorial affairs at which Dada attitudes were clarified and future demonstrations were planned. Sometimes the group would make collective outings to theaters to support plays they approved or to boo and heckle those they disliked. They were also occasionally invited to explain their philosophy to outside groups. This was the kind of challenge the Dadaists most enjoyed. Their aim was generally to bore and insult their audience to the point of revolt, and their criterion of success was the degree of violence they managed to stir up.

At one such dinner, at which they were the guests of a group of Russian émigrés, Josephson was declaiming in German against socialism when the trouble began. He was struck in the eye by a stick of celery as the infuriated diners rose to the assault and was saved from further injury by the restaurant's manager who prudently decided to declare the meeting closed.

Cowley arrived in Paris from Montpellier University in 1922, at about the time that Josephson was leaving it for central Europe. He was a late convert to Dadaism but an enthusiastic one. He was soon an eager apostle of cultural destruction. When Harold Loeb visited him at Giverny one day, he found him in a very anti-literary mood entertaining E. E. Cummings, Dos Passos and the French poet Louis Aragon. By the end of an evening's drinking the friends had become so convinced of the futility of books that, at Cowley's insistence, they started piling heaps of French novels, pamphlets and old copies of the *Nouvelle Revue Française* on the floor and set fire to them. Cummings finally doused the smouldering remains by urinating on them. All of those present at the scene were of course making their living from literature, but Dada thrived on that kind of contradiction.

Aragon's friendship nearly got Cowley into serious trouble the following year. On Bastille Day, 1923, the two of them were sitting in the Dôme with the American artist

Lawrence Vail. The conversation turned to the Rotonde opposite them across the boulevard, and to the misdeeds of its owner. He was said to have been rude to the café's old artist customers and to have insulted several American girls of the Quarter by asking them to leave the café because he considered their dress or behavior immodest. Worst of all, a rumor was circulating that he had acted as a police informer and had betrayed several anarchists.

The thought of this so enraged the three of them that they decided to stage a confrontation. They made their way to the café and demanded to speak to the manager. The waiters, sensing trouble, refused to fetch him, and succeeded in gently manhandling the trio out of the café. Undaunted by this rebuff, they made their way back to the bar, where Aragon, in the Dada manner, began loudly to harangue the other customers. This brought the manager running. Waiters also intervened and in the ensuing scuffle Cowley took a swing at the *patron* catching him on the jaw.

The blow was a tactical mistake. It lost Cowley and his friends the sympathy of the onlookers, for although there was a fine tradition of verbal violence in the Quarter, physical violence was considered crude. Yet the three of them managed to get out of the café unharmed. Cowley, however, made the further mistake of returning to the area later in the evening. He was recognized, pointed out to the police, and arrested. The charge could have been quite serious, though in fact the intervention of his friends, who insisted that he had not been in the café at all that evening, saved him from a sentence. He left France for good a few days after the trial, but by that one blow he had assured himself of a place in the memory of the Dadaists and their heirs for years to come.

Cowley and Josephson were not, in fact, the first Americans to be drawn into the world of Dada. A young painter-photographer from New York beat them to it. Before any of them had left America, he had edited and published the only issue of the country's first Dadaist magazine, complete with a mock authorization from Tristan Tzara. The artist was Man Ray, and he was to become the best known American artist in Paris between the Wars.

When he came to France in 1921, Ray spoke not a word of French and had only one contact in the Paris art world, Marcel Duchamp, with whom he had become friendly in New York. As a young, self-taught painter, Ray's eyes had been opened to the possibilities of modern art by the Armory Show in which Duchamp's *Nude descending a staircase* had been one of the most controversial works. Duchamp had subsequently introduced him to Dadaism, and it was largely as a result of his encouragement that Ray travelled across the Atlantic to track down the avant-garde on its home ground.

The Dadaists immediately accepted him into the group, even though the language barrier at first prevented him from talking with them. His first Parisian exhibition was held in a gallery operated by one of the group, the poet, Philippe Soupault. The whole fraternity turned up for the opening. The gallery ceiling was hidden by a cloud of balloons, massed so tightly that they obscured some of Ray's paintings. The balloons were ceremonially exploded amid much merry-making, and the show was generally considered a great success even though no canvasses were sold.

It did not take Ray very long to discover that this was typical. While reputations could be won with avant-garde works, there was not much of a living to be made from them. Fortunately, he also had some experience as a photographer and was able to fall back on this to provide him with an income. The ultimate irony of Ray's career was that while his reputation in America was primarily that of a Surrealist artist, in France he was better known for his photographic work – in the words of the French writer Maurice Sachs – one of the most talented and best-loved of Parisian photographers.

As a Surrealist, he painted and created objects; the one entitled *Le Cadeau* is typical – an ordinary flat-iron with a menacing row of tacks fixed to the ironing surface. He invented the Rayograph or cameraless photograph, made by placing objects on unexposed photo paper and developing the results. He performed in Surrealist films and stage shows. Francis Picabia made him sit motionless on stage throughout a Swedish Ballet performance, as a living element of decoration. In René Clair's film *Entr'acte*, Marcel Duchamp and he were hosed with water while playing chess on a theater roof.

He also shared the Surrealists' café life and went on their group outings. On one of these, the artists managed to infuriate the population of a Norman village so successfully that they were driven back against a café window in the main square sufficiently violently for it to shatter. Rescue was accomplished only when the local *gendarmes* returned from their Sunday afternoon's fishing.

The girl who caused much of the trouble on that occasion as on many others was Man Ray's mistress, the celebrated Kiki of Montparnasse. Kiki was already a well-known character in the Quarter when he first met her. She had modelled for Modigliani, Foujita and Kisling. Though not conventionally beautiful, her appearance was always striking, partly as a result of her highly original use of make-up, and she was known at least by sight by most of the denizens of artistic Montparnasse.

While her individuality endeared her to artists, it sometimes shocked the conventionally minded. When Ray first met her, she was on the point of being thrown out of a café because the manager considered that she did not look respectable. Ray rescued her by inviting her to join him for a drink. Within minutes of meeting her, he asked her to model for him. At first she was unwilling – he later found out that this was because she had no pubic hair, and did not like to expose what she considered a bizarre defect to the camera's eye – but she eventually consented, and by the end of her second sitting they were lovers. Ray ended up living with her for the next six years.

Kiki turned out to be a faithful but jealous partner. Ray arrived home one day to find that the telephone numbers of all the women in his address book had been disfigured. She was also capable of verbally and even physically attacking girls to whom he paid too much attention at parties. In addition to modelling, she earned her living as an enter-

Left: Lovers of literature and champagne share a glass of bubbly at a small café in Montmartre.

Above: Sculpture students at work in a studio in the Latin Quarter.

tainer in the Montparnasse *boîtes*, singing risqué songs in a low, clear voice accompanied by a suggestive repertoire of expressions and gestures.

With Ray's encouragement, she also took up painting. She held an exhibition of her work in a Montparnasse gallery. The poet Robert Desnos wrote the catalog introduction, and everyone in the Quarter turned up for the opening. Less propitious from Ray's point of view was her decision to write her memoirs. The book was a success, coming out in French and English editions (Hemingway wrote an introduction for the latter) but it marked the end of their relationship; Kiki left him to live with her French publisher.

Ray had, in the meantime, found a new medium to experiment with – 'moving' film. His first cinematic venture was very much of an improvisation. He had filmed only a few seconds' worth of material on a freshly-bought camera when Tristan Tzara, who had heard of his acquisition, came to tell him that a film by him was programmed for a Dada performance three days hence. Ray rose to the challenge. He applied the Rayograph technique to several lengths of

movie film, cut in the material he had already prepared, stuck the whole thing up with tape, and entitled it *The Return to Reason*. He was as curious as the audience on the night of the screening to see how the first Dadaist film would look.

In fact no-one saw very much of it as the tape joins broke while passing through the projector. Enough appeared on the screen, however, to set off the customary Dada riot, and Ray emerged from the incident with an unexpected reputation as an experimental film-maker.

On the strength of this, patrons appeared with funds to finance further explorations. The most exotic of these supporters was the Vicomte de Noailles, who invited Ray to make what was in essence an avant-garde home-movie featuring the Vicomte and his house-guests at his recently built villa in the south of France. Ray devised the basic elements of a plot, and found a title for the film: *Les Mystères du Château du Dé*. To increase the sense of mystery and to preserve the anonymity of his camera-shy actors, Ray suggested that they all should wear stockings over their heads. This tactic proved effective, though it nearly caused the death of his patron who came close to suffocating after submerging in his stocking during a swimming-pool scene. In spite of this mishap, the Viscount was delighted with the film. Ray himself had lost interest in the cinema by that time and refused offers of further work. However it was his film that inspired the Viscount to commission two other experimental classics, Bunuel and Dali's *Un Chien Andalou* and Cocteau's *Sang d'un Poète*.

As a photographer, Ray had access to many different levels of Parisian society. His own interests inclined him towards artists, and he made it his business to see that he had portraits of all the major figures of literature and the fine arts on his files. He photographed Joyce, Hemingway, Pound and Stein; several of his works found their way onto the walls of Sylvia Beach's bookshop. He took an encyclopedist's delight in recording the appearance of all the best painters and sculptors of the Ecole de Paris. And because in Paris, society follows art, he soon found himself in demand as a portrait photographer among the more 'advanced' sections of the aristocracy. The first of his clients was the Marquise Casati, an eccentric and beautiful noblewoman who used to receive guests entwined in a live, twelve-foot python. She enthusiastically admired what Ray considered a spoiled portrait of her because it gave her not one but two pairs of kohl-rimmed eyes. Word of the young American photographer spread quickly through the *beau monde*. The Aga Khan came to be photographed in boxing gloves. Some wealthy women even made discreet enquiries to find out if he would photograph them in the nude.

By the end of the 1930s he was a wealthy man with a studio in Paris, a house in St. Germain and, briefly, an apartment in Antibes. His cars – for he was a motoring enthusiast – were the admiration of the Paris art world. He spent his summers at Mougins in the company of Picasso and Paul Eluard. He had retained the respect of the Surrealists while managing to avoid getting caught up in the theoretical in-fighting of that faction-torn movement. He had a secure income from his photographic work for advertising agencies and fashion magazines, and his artistic reputation was intact. He had also found a new companion, a dancer from Guadeloupe called Adrienne. It was a pleasant, healthy situation for a man who had arrived in the country less than two decades earlier almost penniless and without a word of French.

No other American artist in Paris had comparable critical and material success unless it was the painter Jules Pascin. Though technically American, Pascin was really a citizen of the world. Born in Bulgaria, the son of a Spanish Jewish father and a half-Serbian, half-Italian mother, Pascin (whose real name was Julius Pincas) studied in Berlin, Vienna and Paris before going to the United States. He stayed long enough to become an American citizen, but after the war he returned to Europe, basing himself in Paris. He spent the dozen years of life that remained to him before his tragic and inexplicable suicide in 1930, painting the delicately erotic nudes that made up the major part of his life's work. Though he was friendly with many of the American artists and writers of the Quarter, neither his life nor his painting was fundamentally American. He had chosen his nationality almost by accident, his experience of life in the USA was no greater than his experience in three or four other countries in which he had lived. He hardly even spoke the language.

There was also the sculptor Jo Davidson. Davidson was one of a whole generation of American artists who went to Paris to study in the years before the First World War. However, unlike such pioneers of American modernism as John Marin, Arthur Dove and Charles Demuth who returned to work in America, he decided to return to Paris after the war.

Though he was sufficiently friendly towards modernism to have been one of the organizers of the Armory Show, his own endeavors were in the classic portrait bust tradition. His work between the wars to some extent paralleled Ray's photography for Davidson also was intent on recording the appearance of the writers and artists, as well as the soldiers and statesmen, of his day. He modelled most of the talents of the Quarter, in which he was a popular and well-known figure. It was in his studio that the only meeting between James Joyce and Gertrude Stein took place. The rival gods of modernism could find nothing at all to say to one another.

There was a ready market for Davidson's work, and he was rewarded with a constant flow of commissions. Before

Below left and right: Alexander Calder was an important American painter of circus subjects who lived in Paris in the '20s; his mobiles set a style which is still imitated.

Above: Man Ray visited Picasso (second from right) at the artist's home in Antibes in 1937.

the war he had married a French girl who became a success in her own right as a dress designer with a boutique on the Champs Elysées. Between the two of them, they were able to afford a chateaù in the Touraine, where they entertained an extraordinarily wide circle of friends that stretched from the journalist Lincoln Steffens, who wrote part of his autobiography there, to the novelists H. G. Wells and Arnold Bennett and the millionaire Otto Kahn. By the thirties, Davidson's services were equally in demand in Europe and the United States, and his 'imaginary museum' of portrait busts included most of the great celebrities of his day.

Like Man Ray, Jo Davidson was a part of an expatriate tradition in American art that stretched back into the nineteenth century. Their predecessors in Paris included Whistler who had studied and worked there, and the Impressionist, Mary Cassatt, a pupil of Degas who survived in lonely isolation in her chateau near Beauvais until 1926. Yet their experience was far from typical of the twenties. Though there was never any shortage of American artists in Montparnasse, no expatriate movement equivalent to the Lost Generation in *literature* came into being.

There was of course a constant stream of young artists arriving to study in Paris, and of older talents returning to refresh their inspiration. There were groups who met regularly in the cafés of the Quarter; as Davidson remarked, "an artist just didn't stay in his studio and work – he had to talk. Talking was part of it." They even exhibited together. One group was associated with Samuel Putnam's *New Review*. Feelings between this group and the more conservative American painters of the Quarter ran high. On one

occasion Joseph Stella, the leading figure among the modernist faction, came to blows with a couple of his fellow-countrymen in the Dôme. The rival painters dueled with canes and with café chairs until the police were called to break up the fight.

Yet the Americans never made much collective impact on the Paris art scene. For painters like Stella, a stay in the city was simply one stage in an essentially American career. Those American artists who did achieve a kind of fame in the Quarter generally did so for extraneous reasons, like Eugene McCown, who was known for his jazz piano-playing at the Boeuf sur le Toît, or Hilaire Hiler, who decorated and for a time ran the famous Jockey Club, which Hemingway was later to describe nostalgically as "the best night-club that ever was".

Yet Paris continued to dominate the thinking of the American art world until after the Second World War. It was, after all, a world capital of painting in a way that no city had been since Rome in the seventeenth century. Everything of any importance in the fine arts happened in Paris. Painters could go there, accept or even reject its influence. They could react like George Biddle, who noted in his memoirs: "It dawned on me, at the end of three years, that my natural predilection for something a little different was simply that I was American;" or like Thomas Hart Benton, who in later life growled about his four-year stay in Paris, "I wallowed in every cockeyed *ism* that came along, and it took me ten years to get all that modern is dirt out of my system." But they ignored it at their peril.

The situation in music was, by 1920, not very different from that in art. Throughout the nineteenth century Germany and Austria had dominated the musical world, but with the ebbing of Romanticism their rule no longer went un-

challenged. The Impressionism of Debussy and Ravel had
initially drawn attention to Paris, while the playful anarchy
of Eric Satie's music had struck at the very roots of the
intense German tradition. "After the war the center of
musical activity definitely shifted from Germany to
France," Aaron Copland wrote retrospectively. "The
gradual swing away from Central Europe had been gaining
momentum ever since 1900, and by 1920 Paris was the
leading spirit in all new musical things."

This swing was reflected in the lives of the American
composers and musicians of the period. Because the
development of musical culture had, in the nineteenth
century, lagged behind the other arts in America, the
tradition of pursuing musical studies abroad was deeply
embedded. The musically minded had long ago got into the
habit of travelling to Europe in search of employment or
inspiration. The list of nineteenth century exiles included
picturesque figures like the songwriter John Howard Payne,
who composed "Home, Sweet Home" in a fit of nostalgia
in a cheap apartment in the Palais Royal while struggling to
earn a living as an actor-dramatist on the Paris stage.

The tendency before the First World War had, however,
been to go to Germany. One of the first to go against it was
Aaron Copland, who chose instead to go to a newly opened
music school for Americans in Fontainebleau when he
started his musical *wanderjahre* in 1921.

It was there that he met Nadia Boulanger. She was then
an unknown 33-year-old teaching harmony, a subject that
Copland had already explored to his own satisfaction.
However he was so impressed by her enthusiasm and her
knowledge of music that he persuaded her to instruct him
privately in composition. She left her mark on Copland as
she was to leave it on a whole generation of American
composers. Apart from her innate talents as a teacher, she
had a firm belief in the future of American music that was
shared by few of her compatriots. She was convinced that a
national school was about to appear in the United States
rather as the Russian school had emerged in the late
nineteenth century, and she communicated her confidence to
the Americans who studied with her. There were to be
many of these, for her reputation spread quickly in musical
circles; but Copland always claimed to have been the first
of them.

If that was so, then the second or third was Virgil
Thomson. Like Copland, he arrived in Paris in 1921, on a
one-year travelling fellowship from Harvard. Originally
from Kansas City, he later said that he chose to live in Paris
(where he settled in 1925) because it reminded him of his
home town – adding that, because Paris is so cosmopolitan, anyone can find an image of his origins in it.

Paris was a hotbed of advice, tuition and influences, but it
was not an easy place for an American composer to earn a
living. The musical world was riven with cliques and
coteries (the predominant one being that of the Six, the
group associated with Jean Cocteau); but none of these had
time to listen to the works of young, unknown artists from a
distant country that had no recognized musical tradition.
Yet even if opportunities to have one's work performed
were hard to come by, the atmosphere of the city was
friendly for creators of any kind. As Thomson used to say,
even the police treated you well if you were an artist.

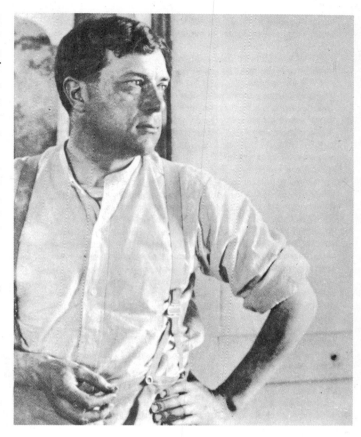

Above: Georges Braque in 1922. Braque was a cubist
contemporary of Picasso but not nearly as influential.

Copland avoided the problem of winning a Paris reputation by returning to America, to test his first compositions
on a native audience. Thomson eked out the lean year
before his reputation was established on the precarious
charity of friends and patrons. Other composers and
musicians survived, in the affluent twenties, on money
from home. The artist's life was fortunately not an expensive
one.

Only one American managed to make an immediate
impact on the Paris musical world – a brash young man
from New Jersey called George Antheil. Before his arrival
in Paris in 1923, he had already made a successful concert
tour of central Europe and of Germany, where the
premier of his First Symphony had been conducted by the
former flying ace Schultz von Dornberg with the Berlin
Philharmonic. He had also written a series of extremely
avant-garde piano pieces, which he performed himself,
sometimes to less than ecstatic audiences. In fact one of his
concerts in Budapest had ended in a riot. Undaunted, he
had returned to the concert hall the following evening
sporting a .32 automatic. Ordering the ushers to lock the
doors of the hall, he placed the gun ostentatiously on top of
the piano before sitting down to play. The audience that
evening listened to his performance in attentive silence.

In Paris, Antheil and his Hungarian wife moved into the
empty flat above Sylvia Beach's bookshop, thereby gaining
an immediate entrée into the expatriate literary world.
Writers calling in at Shakespeare and Company got into the
habit of also visiting the young composer upstairs, and soon
his small flat had all the allures of a first-rate literary salon.
He claims in his memoirs to have once entertained a teatime

Right and below: Two scenes from *Four Saints in Three Acts,* text by Gertrude Stein and music by Virgil Thomson, were first performed in New York by an all-black cast.

gathering that included Joyce, Ezra Pound, Ford Madox Ford, Ernest Hemingway and two visitors from England – T. S. Eliot and Wyndham Lewis.

For a musician, he led a surprisingly literary life. Through his German connections he had been appointed the Paris representative of a magazine called *Der Querschnitt*, whose editor, a certain Count von Wedderkop, he christened Mr. Awfully Nice from the only two English words he was ever heard to utter. On the advice of Ezra Pound and Sylvia Beach, he sent the magazine first the poems of Joyce's *Chamber Music*, and then some of Hemingway's early short stories, which thus appeared in German translation before any publisher had been found for them in English. He became a close friend of Joyce who at one time talked of writing a libretto for him. They shared a taste for Purcell's operas, and on hearing that one was to be performed privately in Paris, the two of them gatecrashed the event – and were unceremoniously asked to leave when their hostess realized that they had not been invited.

It was Ezra Pound, though, who was to have the most significant effect on his career. When Antheil met him, Pound was entering a musical phase. Besides learning to play the bassoon, he had been studying harmony and trying his hand at composition. Pound was a born founder of schools and encourager of talents, and the appearance of a young, avant-garde composer who also happened to be American was too good an opportunity for him to miss. He adopted Antheil's music and set about launching its composer in the Paris music world. He took away some random jottings that Antheil had made about music, and to the composer's astonishment came back with a pamphlet entitled *Antheil and the Theory of Harmony*. He organized a couple of recitals at which Antheil's and his own music was performed by another Pound *protégée*, the violinist Olga Rudge. At Pound's insistence, Antheil was even allowed to have a piano in his flat – something Sylvia Beach had previously forbidden.

Antheil was never entirely happy with this burst of patronage. He felt that Pound's aggressive championing of his cause antagonized other critics, and he wrote later that "from the first day I met him Ezra was never to have even the slightest idea of what I was really after in music". However he was swept along in a maelstrom of activity that included an invitation from Rolf de Maré, then Diaghilev's principal rival, to perform a prelude for his Ballets Suédois. This performance was well attended by the expatriate intelligentsia – including T. S. Eliot, who came over from London – and turned into a classically Parisian theater riot. Fist-fights broke out in the hall between Antheil's supporters and detractors, and someone in the gallery started dropping chairs on the heads of spectators in the orchestra below.

This kind of reception was then regarded, of course, as a mark of musical success, and Antheil's reputation seemed to be made. Other patrons began to take an interest in his work. His principal supporter was the American heiress, Mrs. Christian Gross who became a 'sugar' mammy for the new American music – literally so, as it was from the sugar trade that her fortune had come. She was then married to the First Secretary of the American Embassy and her luxurious flat on the Champ de Mars became a testing-ground for the new American music where premières of works by Antheil and Virgil Thomson were held. It was in her salon that Antheil's most celebrated piece, the *Ballet Mécanique*, was first performed. Scored for eight pianos, it proved so noisy in the enclosed space of a large drawing-room that the only sensation that most of its hearers felt was one of physical pain.

Antheil's career reached a climax with the successful performance of his Second Symphony at the Théâtre des Champs Elysées in 1926. From that point onwards things started to go wrong for him. His patroness, Mrs. Gross, gave up her salon, along with her husband and children, to elope with a Mexican. Antheil himself contracted pneumonia and had to go to Chamonix to recuperate. A piano concerto that he wrote there flopped in Paris. His style had swung towards neo-classicism; critics who had admired what they considered the American brashness of his jazz-influenced music were no longer so impressed when he began working in a European idiom. His *Ballet Mécanique* was staged amid much ballyhoo at Carnegie Hall, complete with aeroplane propellers on stage that ruffled the coiffures of ladies in the stalls and sent at least one wig flying. But New York was not impressed. One review was headlined "50 million Frenchmen can be wrong". Antheil became so depressed that friends, convinced he was suffering from tuberculosis, packed him off to an expensive clinic in the Pyrenees. He returned with a clean bill of health, but Paris was no longer so welcoming, so in 1928 he left for Germany, where he had been commissioned to write an opera.

While Antheil's career was faltering, Thomson's was picking up steam. Where Antheil had fallen in with the Joyce-Pound coterie, Thomson had given his allegiance to Gertrude Stein – in those days the choice between the two tended to be exclusive. Thomson cemented his friendship with Miss Stein by setting her pieces, *Susie Asado* and *Preciosilla*, to music. He introduced his friends to her salon: the poet Georges Hugnet, the painters Christian Bérard and Eugène Berman. She christened them 'the young men of 26', for that was the age that most of them appeared to be, and for a time these Neo-Romantics dominated her social life in the way that the Cubists had done before the First World War. Thomson soon found himself "serving Gertrude Stein as translator, impressario, music setter and literary agent". In return she championed his music and sought patrons for him from amongst the millionaires she knew.

In fact Thomson's financial status had already considerably improved. The mother of a wealthy friend was providing him with a steady F.3,000 a month. He had found a permanent home at 17, quai Voltaire, in a fifth-storey walk-up flat from which he could look out at the Seine, the Louvre, the Opéra, and, in the distance, Sacré Coeur. He could afford to eat regularly at a pleasant little restaurant in the rue Jacob called, with foresight, *La Quatrième République*; at that time France was still living under the Third. He ordered his clothes from Lanvin, had his dinners sent up from a hotel a quarter of a mile away, and hired a Russian gymnast to keep him in good physical shape. It was, for a young composer, a comfortable and civilized life that he was to describe later as "the generally hygienic Paris routine – to bed by midnight and up by eight, love-making chiefly in the afternoon, with two tasty

Below: Young American composers who were in Paris in 1926 to study under Nadia Boulanger. Left to right: Thomson, Ellwell, Walter Piston and Aaron Copland. Along with Gershwin, they represented the finest in American serious music composed between the wars.

meals a day, some calisthenics, lots of walking, a little wine, no hard liquor and no telephone."

His music was also being heard. In 1928, the year in which Antheil left Paris, the first concert devoted entirely to his works was staged in the Old Conservatory, near the Folies Bergère, in front of an audience that included Nadia Boulanger, Jean Cocteau, and of course Gertrude Stein. It attracted attention, but failed to bring in any commissions. Thomson then began working on the musical portraits of friends that were to be one of the most distinctive features of his *oeuvre*, and also put the finishing touches to the most substantial result of his collaboration with Gertrude Stein, the opera, *Four Saints in Three Acts*.

This was to be the work that finally made his name. Its première in Hartford, Connecticut, in 1934 was a critical and social triumph that launched Thomson's reputation in the United States and at the same time confirmed Stein's. It was subsequently staged in New York and Chicago, and the wave of interest that it aroused was sufficient to keep Thomson in America for the better part of the next four years. It was not until 1938 that he moved permanently back to Paris, where he just had time to complete his book, *The State of Music*, before his career, like so many others, was interrupted by the coming of the war.

Antheil had made the journey home long before the Nazi storm-clouds gathered. He had returned to Paris briefly in 1930, to find his old apartment above Shakespeare and Company occupied by royalty. Crown Prince Norodeth of Cambodia, a democratically minded young man who was using his royal allowance to support several dozen of his compatriots through their studies in Paris, was renting it. Though by regal standards the Crown Prince was slumming, and he dignified the place with a fine Cézanne, a luxurious oriental carpet and a grand piano.

After a final European visit on a Guggenheim scholarship in 1932, when he chose to live in Cagnes-sur-Mer, an artists' colony on the Riviera, Antheil decided to return to the United States for good. He spent the thirties and the war years in an odd variety of occupations that included writing film scores for Cecil B. de Mille, authoring a syndicated column of advice for the love-lorn entitled *Boy advises Girl*, writing a book of accurate political prophesy called *The Shape of the War to Come*, and co-patenting a design for a radio-controlled torpedo with Hedy Lamarr, a friend of his in Hollywood. He also continued to compose his own music, but he never recaptured the originality of his Paris days.

The fact is that for all of Antheil's and Thomson's efforts there was never a Paris school of American music, any more than there was of American painting. Paris was an influence, a place to study, or, for those like Thomson who stayed, a comfortable and convenient place to work. In the long run, however, the reputations of the American artists of the inter-war generation were not made there but in New York. Those artists who failed to convert the promise of early success in Paris into the solid currency of New York backing soon saw the enthusiasm of Paris audiences drain away into indifference. In some ways, Antheil's career paralleled that

Left : George Antheil returning home to his flat above Sylvia Beach's Shakespeare and Company.

Above: The rue de l'Odéon as seen from Adrienne Monnier's window above Shakespeare and Co.

Above : George Antheil.

of the writer Robert McAlmon, another young man with a future that never quite materialized. And he would no doubt have sympathized with McAlmon's bitter judgement of the city that feted him and then forgot him: "I knew all too well that Paris is a bitch, and that one shouldn't become infatuated with bitches, particularly when they have wit, imagination, experience, and tradition behind their ruthlessness."

6. Heroes and Heroines

At first it seemed as though the twenties had no need of heroes. Too many had been lost in the war, and yet the world had not become a better place to live in. The mood was disenchanted and cynical. In the euphoria of peace noble intentions seemed expendable. The great men were dead or, like Hemingway's characters, drinking. In their place the newspapers made do with film stars and foreign royalty. So when, one night in May, 1927, a 25-year-old stunt flyer and airmail pilot from the Midwest came down into the spotlights of world publicity, he found a world starved of grand gestures waiting to welcome him.

Charles Lindbergh always disliked the nickname 'Lucky', but on his great transatlantic flight, fortune was certainly on his side. How else to explain the fact that, without any premeditation on his part, *The Spirit of St. Louis* touched down at exactly 10.24 p.m. on a Saturday evening? It was precisely the moment when Parisians, in the best of after dinner moods, are looking for something amusing to do with the weekend. Even if the flight had been planned by a battalion of public relations men, the timing could not have been bettered. Had his take-off from Roosevelt Field, Long Island, the previous morning been delayed for another five or six hours by adverse weather conditions and had he landed at three or four a.m., perhaps only a few hundred people would have waited up to greet him. Of course, his exploit would still have won the admiration of the world and he would still have been treated as a hero; but perhaps the peculiar note of crowd hysteria that, from the moment of his landing, was to become associated with his name would never have developed.

However, there were 100,000 or so festive, wined-and-dined Parisians waiting at Le Bourget as the small plane circled above the airport and then swooped down on the

Left: Lindbergh in his *Spirit of St Louis* above Paris after his famous flight.
Below: Lindbergh and his plane which captured the imagination of two continents.

Left: Charles A. Lindbergh is greeted by crowds at Le Bourget airport in Paris after he completed his solo flight across the Atlantic.

Below: *Spirit of St Louis* on Curtiss Field in New Jersey prior to take-off.

Right: A headline which was repeated across the front pages of every newspaper in the world in 1927.

Left: Throngs gather in front of Paris' Hôtel de Ville to greet Lindbergh (encircled).
Above: The shy pilot (left) leaves the Elysée Palace after a wildly enthusiastic welcome.

Above: Lindbergh's hand is shaken by the Foreign Minister of France, Aristide Briand.
Above right: Marshal Foch congratulates Lindbergh.

flare-lit runway. The plane touched down smoothly; after $33\frac{1}{2}$ hours of uninterrupted flying, Lindbergh was again on land. He turned the plane to taxi back to the hangars only to find, to his astonishment, that a cheering mob was running at full speed towards him. A cordon of police and two companies of soldiers with bayonets fixed had been completely insufficient to hold back the spectators. He cut the engine at once to avoid injuring anyone, and, with the sense of unreality felt by anyone who has stayed awake too long, soon found himself surrounded by a sea of faces laughing, crying and shouting at him in a language he did not understand. Worried for the safety of the plane, he tried to climb down from it, but no sooner had his leg emerged from the cockpit than it was seized by wellwishers who pulled him bodily out.

For the better part of half an hour Lindbergh was carried backwards and forwards on the shoulders of the crowd. He was quite unable to rescue himself—or indeed to do anything at all. Two French aviators finally came to his aid. Seizing his flying helmet, they placed it on the head of an American journalist named Harry Wheeler and shouted to the crowd that he was Lindbergh. In the diversion this

caused, they were able to hurry Lindbergh away to the safety of a hangar. Poor Wheeler, his angry protestations only further convincing the crowd of his authenticity, was carried back in triumph to the airport buildings. It was only when he was presented to US Ambassador Myron T. Herrick that he finally managed to explain the mistake.

Lindbergh's first concern was for the safety of his plane. It was eventually rescued from the crowd by police and soldiers and taken to a hangar. Though it had been man-handled by souvenir hunters, only superficial damage was done. The principal loss was that of the log book of the flight, which Lindbergh never recovered. Some canvas sections had been torn from the wing, but the damage was quickly repaired by a French company which offered its services to Lindbergh free of charge. The plane's assailants got their mementos cheaply; when the company subsequently auctioned for charity four strips of fabric removed during the repairs, they fetched a total of F.76,000, two of the buyers being the Comte de Chavagnac and the dramatist Henry Bernstein.

It was not until two hours after touch-down that the real Lindbergh reached Ambassador Herrick. With a self-deprecating grin he handed over the letters of introduction he had brought with him in case the ambassador should not know his name. Apart from five sandwiches, only one of which he had eaten, these had been almost the only personal

articles he had brought with him. He accepted an invitation to stay at the Embassy. By the time he arrived there he had been without sleep for forty hours, but he was still sufficiently keyed up by his reception to talk to waiting journalists. "I could have flown half the distance again," he said, then added modestly, "You know, flying a good airplane doesn't require nearly as much attention as a motor car."

One reason for the warmth of Lindbergh's reception in France was that his success was almost totally unexpected. Of the three principal contenders for the Orteig Prize – $25,000 first offered eight years previously by an American hotel owner for the first New York-to-Paris flight – Lindbergh had seemed to have the least hope. He had neither the experience of Commander Byrd, whose flight to the North Pole had made headlines the year before, nor the financial backing of Clarence Chamberlin, with his sophisticated Bellanca plane. Above all, Lindbergh's decision to fly alone – both of his rivals had two-seater planes – had seemed like a foolhardy stunt certain to doom him to failure. After all, four Americans had already died in tests for the transatlantic flight and the general opinion was that Lindbergh would be extremely lucky not to join them.

The French were particularly concerned at the time of Lindbergh's flight with the fate of their compatriots, Nungesser and Coli, who had attempted to make the flight in reverse, from Paris to New York. Their plane had disappeared somewhere over the Atlantic, and all attempts to locate it and the pilots had failed. Hope for the two aviators had not been entirely abandoned by the time Lindbergh took off, though in fact they were never to be found. Premature celebrations of a French triumph had turned to a mood of bitterness when the plane failed to reach New York. Rumors that American authorities had helped sabotage the flight by withholding necessary weather information were rife. Feelings were in fact running so high that Ambassador Herrick had cabled from Paris, only a few days before Lindbergh's departure: "The take-off of a transatlantic flight from the United States at this time when the fate of the French aviators is still in doubt, might be misunderstood and misinterpreted."

Given the habitual touchiness of the French to questions of national prestige, the reception they accorded to Lindbergh was, under the circumstances, all the more moving. The enthusiasm was by no means limited to the thousands of Parisians who had crowded out to Le Bourget, jamming the roads between the airport and Paris. In the city itself, crowds had packed into the Place de l'Opéra to watch the latest news bulletins flash over an advertising hoarding. At Zelli's and Florence's, two American owned Montmartre night clubs, champagne was on the house that night for visitors. Josephine Baker stopped the show at the Folies

Bergère to announce the news of his arrival. In bars and on the street, tourists were toasted and congratulated by total strangers on the strength of their compatriot's exploit. It was an extraordinary outburst of popular emotion.

And it was only a beginning. For the week in which Lindbergh remained in Paris the city belonged to him. The day after his arrival the Stars and Stripes flew all day long above the French Ministry of Foreign Affairs – the first time that this honor had ever been accorded to a foreign visitor who was not a head of state. Even some of the city's tramcars flew the American flag. Lindbergh was awarded the medal of the Legion of Honor by President Doumergue, and was invited to address both the Senate and the National Assembly. At a charity benefit at the Théâtre des Champs-Elysées, his autograph was auctioned for $1,500.

The celebrations reached their climax with an official reception at the Hôtel de Ville on Ascension Day, a French national holiday, when nearly half a million Parisians were in the streets to watch Lindbergh's triumphal progress. There was wild enthusiasm among the 40,000 spectators packed into the Place de l'Hôtel de Ville when Lindbergh appeared on the balcony above them holding the Stars and Stripes and the *tricoleur* in his hand. When he re-emerged from the building after the ceremony, the crowd broke through police lines to run after the car.

Lindbergh's triumph was almost eerily perfect. It is hard to find a satisfactory rational explanation for the veneration he aroused. There were one or two fortuitous elements in it, besides the timing of his arrival. The name of his plane, *The Spirit of St. Louis*, automatically recalled, for the French, not the American city, but their own crusader king after whom the city was named. Yet by far the most important thing was Lindbergh himself. His personality and behavior transformed a memorable feat of aviation into the theme for a prolonged burst of international hysteria. Though totally unprepared for the role he was called upon to play, he did not make a single false step. His least action seemed to heighten and embellish the Lindbergh legend: the long-distance telephone call to his mother in Detroit the morning after his arrival; the visit to Mme. Nungesser, mother of the lost flyer, in which he offered words of encouragement to the weeping woman; the smiling meeting with Louis Blériot, France's cross-Channel pioneer of twenty years before; the brief, self-deprecating speeches he made at the innumerable ceremonial banquets given in his honor. No Hollywood casting director could have improved on his rumpled, boyish appearance; no scriptwriter could have bettered his improvised acts and words.

He was to repeat his faultless performance in Belgium and England before the cruiser *Memphis*, dispatched specially by President Coolidge, arrived at Cherbourg to take him and his plane home. By that time the idea of Lindbergh as America's 'ambassador without portfolio' was firmly entrenched. Franco-American relations were at a low point before his arrival. The collapse of the franc had had created an atmosphere of recrimination that had been aggravated by America's insistence that France repay her war debts. For the French press, Uncle Sam had become Uncle Shylock, demanding his pound of flesh while continuing to hamper France's efforts to collect reparations from Germany acknowledged by the Treaty of Versailles.

It was against this dark political background that Lindbergh succeeded in bringing thousands of Frenchmen out into the streets waving the Stars and Stripes.

But the public mood changes fast in France, and within three months of Lindbergh's departure the country was shaken by the worst anti-American rioting of the decade. Crowds invaded the expatriate cafés on the boulevard du Montparnasse, jostling the customers and throwing chairs and tables into the street. For an entire month a platoon of fifty policemen had to be stationed outside the American Embassy where Lindbergh had been cheered, to protect it and its staff from attack. Though Lindbergh's own popularity remained intact, the execution of the shoemaker Nicola Sacco and the fishmonger Bartolomeo Vanzetti in Charlestown, Massachusetts, for a crime they had not committed, lost America almost all of the political good-will that, by his skill and daring, he had so laboriously won.

There was to be nothing to compare with Lindbergh's triumph between the Armistice and the Liberation celebrations in 1944. In a way, the welcome given to Lindbergh recalled the best days of Franco-American co-operation in the First World War. Many of his older admirers among the Parisian crowds must have reflected that it was the aviators of the Escadrille Lafayette, who had been among the first Americans to rally to the cause of France in 1916.

Yet there were other Americans whose exploits temporarily caught the imagination of the French and who won for themselves briefer moments of glory. One was Gertrude Ederle, a New York butcher's daughter, whose ambition was to be the first woman to swim the English Channel. She tried twice in 1925, but failed each time. However, with backing from the *New York Daily News*, she returned to France the following year to prepare herself for what the writer Paul Gallico was later to call "the greatest recorded athletic feat by a woman in the history of the world."

She went into training at Cap Gris-Nez, under the supervision of an Englishman, William Burgess who was one of five men who had swum the Channel – in his case after eighteen attempts. Gertrude's third attempt was planned for August, when the cold and choppy Channel waters were as warm as they were ever likely to be.

She wore a two-piece black silk bathing suit for the swim, removing the top once in the water. More important was the three-layer coating of unguents that covered her body to protect her from the cold: first a layer of olive oil, then one of lanoline, and finally a mixture of vasoline and lard.

From Cap Gris-Nez her objective was Dover, a little more than twenty miles away by boat on England's Kent coast. For a swimmer, however, at the mercy of waves and currents, the distance is almost doubled. The weather, which had been good when she set out, changed in mid-Channel, and for a time it seemed as if she was fated to fail once again. Three miles from the English coast, her father hailed her from the back-up boat to ask if she wanted to quit. "What for?" she shouted back through the mist.

Above right: Gertrude Ederle is given a final greasing before her Channel swim.
Right: Lillian Cannon, who planned a similar feat a year before, wishes Ederle bon voyage.

Above: Ederle at Cap Gris Nez.
Above right: Ederle steps into the cold Channel waters.
Right: Ederle's triumph.

Beacons had been lit along the English coast to guide her home. When she finally reached land at Kingsdown, north of Dover, she learned that she had made the crossing in 14 hours, 31 minutes, and so had not merely become the first woman to achieve the feat but had also clipped nearly two and a half hours off the previous best male time. She got into the boat to sail to Dover, where a reception committee was waiting to celebrate her triumph – only to be held up for three hours at the customs office there because she had no passport with her to enter Britain.

Despite this bureaucratic slight, she was the hero of the hour in France and Britain, and she returned home to a wildly enthusiastic welcome in New York. At a reception in her honor at City Hall, Mayor Jimmy Walker compared her crossing of the Channel to Moses crossing the Red Sea, Caesar crossing the Rubicon and Washington crossing the Delaware, and as a special mark of favor, her father even gave her permission to bob her hair. But Gertrude's moment of glory was short-lived. The newspapers soon found other names to fill their headlines, and by the time

of Lindbergh's flight just nine months later, she had slipped from the public's memory. When a reporter asked her what advice she would give the new hero, she said to take all the opportunities offered because in a few months' time the offers will have stopped coming.

As a twenty-year-old ex-hero she was speaking from experience, but her negative attitude was not what reporters were looking for in the bright dawn of Lindbergh's idealism. The newspapers were to be happier the following year with the exploits of the heavyweight boxer Gene Tunney, who managed a more gracious exit from the spotlight by retiring undefeated as heavyweight champion of the world. He continued to provide good copy by celebrating his retirement with a well-publicized walking tour of Europe in the unlikely company of the writer Thornton Wilder.

Tunney and Wilder had become friendly some years earlier when the two happened to be vacationing at Miami Beach at the same time. Wilder was no doubt intrigued by Tunney's oft-repeated admiration for his fellow-dramatist William Shakespeare. Tunney, for his part, had long had literary leanings, and doubtless found the company of the scholarly dramatist a pleasant contrast to the boxers, trainers and fight organizers with whom he had spent most of his life. Whatever the motives for their friendship, it

QUEEN OF THE WAVES

Above: Gertrude Ederle after her spectacular feat.

Above: Gene Tunney, heavyweight champion in 1926.
Right: Isadora Duncan, the bizarre American dancer, on the terrace of the Château de Bellevue.

provided just the kind of 'silly season' copy that editors enjoy, and even *The New York Times* considered their travel plans front-page news.

They spent two weeks in Paris before heading south. Wilder introduced Tunney to the civilized delights of the capital and to some sections of its literary life. Janet Flanner, in *The New Yorker*, reported a visit that the two had made to the Brasserie Lipp, where the normally imperturbable waiters forgot their other customers' orders and the cashier, awed, stopped making change. The ex-champion, "nervously doffing and donning his hat as if the bay-leaves irked him", talked loudly and intelligently for half an hour, then left.

He was even more ill at ease at a gathering brought together in his honor by Wilder in the Ritz Bar. Among the guests was a slightly tipsy Scott Fitzgerald. Fitzgerald started behaving noisily, bestowing lavish and somewhat patronizing compliments on a beautiful table companion whose husband, the Dean of the Yale Law School, was also in the group. Given his admiration for sporting heroes, he was probably only trying to impress Tunney. The lady, however, took offence, revealing her opinion of him in no uncertain terms. Tunney, embarrassed, walked out.

The 'walking tour' in fact turned into a leisurely car ride from Paris to Rome, where Tunney was to be married. Like the discriminating tourists that they were, Wilder and he zigzagged through France, visiting Chamonix to admire Mont Blanc, and Arles to trace the footsteps of Van Gogh. They watched bull-fighting in the Roman arena at Nîmes, one of a handful of French cities where the sport is allowed by special dispensation. There was nothing very unusual about where they went or what they did, but Tunney's presence ensured that wherever they were they were the focus of attention. In comparison, Wilder's presence was barely noticed. In terms of publicity, the boxing glove proved mightier than the pen.

Boxing, of course, arouses world-wide interest, and a world heavyweight champion is international news. Other varieties of American sports heroes attracted less attention abroad. "This ain't much of a city," growled Babe Ruth after three days of non-recognition in the Paris streets. The final insult to baseball's greatest hitter came when the American Embassy included his name in a long list of recipients of unclaimed mail published in the *Herald Tribune*, just like that of any tourist. "How do you like them guys?" he snorted. "Taking an ad in the paper to find out where the hell I am! That could never happen in New York."

Even heroes and heroines grow old. By the time of the Armistice, the most famous American woman in Europe was on the threshold of middle age. Isadora Duncan, young goddess of the dance, turned forty on May 27, 1918. Though in the nine years that remained to her she was to continue to live her life on a different scale to that of other human beings, the great days of her early triumphs were over. There was an elegiac quality about her final years in France. In spirit she was as generously extravagant as ever, but the body was no longer young. To a generation that had never seen her dance, she seemed in her last years merely a wreck of the woman they had imagined her to be.

Below : Isadora Duncan at Bellevue.
Left : Raymond Duncan, who was as bizarre if not as talented as his sister.
Right : Isadora Duncan in an unusually tranquil pose.

Nonetheless, the influence of her dancing and her life was still very much felt. She had carried the ideals of a pure Byronic romantic into the twentieth century and thereby had created something new. It could be argued that she had done as much to shape her time as her contemporary and spiritual opposite, Henry Ford. He pioneered the machine age, but Isadora re-invented the human form and that influence extended into many different walks of life. Her bare legs and free-flowing robes helped end the tyranny of the corset and petticoat, and through their effect on such dress designers as Paul Poiret foreshadowed the close-fitting, comfortable dresses of our day. The art of eurhythmics grew out of her dancing style, and the idea of physical education through movement was born. She helped to revolutionize traditional concepts of dancing through her influence on the Ballets Russes. In sculpture she inspired Rodin, Maillol and Bourdelle. Her espousal of the cause of free love, her refusal to marry, her careful and conscious choice of the different fathers for her three children, directly challenged nineteenth-century sexual morality.

Isadora was one of the originals of the twentieth century, but it was mainly other people who took advantage of her ideas. By 1918 little of her own was left to her; she had squandered everything in her life except her talent. Fortunes gleaned from her performances and her admirers had been spent as soon as she received them, usually on the children of her beloved dancing school whom she had led around Europe and America for fourteen years in search of a permanent home. Nothing had come of the Temple of the Dance she had started to build in Athens. Her millionaire lover Paris Singer had, in 1913, bought the vast mansion of Bellevue overlooking the Seine near Paris for her and her pupils but with the coming of the war she had lent it to the French government for use as a hospital. By 1918, after four years of military occupation, it was a ruin. Lacking the money to restore it, she sold it to the French government, who wanted to use it to manufacture poison gas.

The most personal and tragic loss of all had been the death of her own two children, drowned when the car in which they had been left rolled down a slope into the Seine. Her third baby died at birth a year later in 1914.

The school, to which Isadora had devoted so much of her time and money, finally broke up in 1920 after the sale of Bellevue. It was during this fallow period when the life's work she had chosen seemed to have come to nothing, that she received an invitation from the Bolshevik government of Russia to make her school there. She accepted, and so began her life's last great adventure.

Isadora knew little and cared less about politics, but the idea of revolution was one that had always appealed to her passionate temperament. She was a revolutionary romantic. Many of her greatest dances had been inspired by hymns of liberation – the *Marseillaise*, which she danced wrapped in a French *tricolor*; the *Marche Slav*, which she used to express the subjection of the Russian serf. She thought that in a country where the old social order had been destroyed, it might be possible for mankind to free itself from the shackles of the past and to make a fresh start. She visualized an entire society constructed in her image, whose children –

Left: Isadora leaves a car like the one in which she died.

the children she was to teach in her state-supported school – would be free to live, to dance and to love as they chose.

It was a glorious illusion, and it gave her the courage to live for the better part of three years in the war-ravaged land. However, she soon lost her faith in the Bolshevik leaders. Finding them gathered in evening dress at what seemed to her a second-rate imitation of a Paris salon, she cried out that they were bourgeois and interrupted the singer who was entertaining them to dance her vision of a revolutionary culture. In spite of this incident, they provided her with a building and funds for her school. She had no difficulty attracting pupils as desperate mothers eager to provide their half-starved children with sustenance, begged her to accept them. For the rest of her stay in Russia she was to divide her time between the care and instruction of the children whom she educated under conditions of real privation, and *tournées* in the Russian provinces. Travelling in fourth-class railway carriages, staying in flea-ridden hotels and boarding houses, sometimes not even finding a roof under which to spend the night, she managed to continue. In terms of endurance it was an achievement.

In Russia, where the marriage laws were lax enough to win her approval, she also found her only husband. Sergei Esenin was a poet of the people, an inspired and half-crazed peasant who wrote revolutionary verse. It was in his company that she made her final, tragi-comic American tour, scandalizing Boston by baring her breasts to the audience and performing in Indianapolis under the watchful gaze of policemen stationed on stage to prevent a similar occurrence. The couples' troubles continued when they stopped in Paris on the way back to Russia. Esenin, who was by then drinking heavily, smashed up their room at the hotel Crillon and was arrested. Isadora was asked to leave the hotel. Later he ran amok at a party at his wife's studio in the rue de la Pompe. Hurling insults at the guests whom he claimed had woken him, he seized a candelabra and flung it at a large ornamental mirror. Several male guests managed to restrain him while a servant called the police. He was led away muttering, "*Bon politzie! Aller avec vous!*" and spent the rest of his stay in Paris in a private mental home.

Isadora eventually took him back to Russia with her, but he abandoned her soon after their return. Two years later he committed suicide; his last act had been to scrawl a message of reconciliation to Isadora in his own blood.

After spending a final year in Russia, Isadora decided to return to France. But she no longer had a passport – the Russian government had failed to return it. She was only able to get a visa to re-enter the country where she had triumphed twenty years before through the personal intervention of her friend, the actress Cécile Sorel. She had saved nothing for her return, and for the last three years of her life was to live in a succession of borrowed rooms and luxury hotels in which her stay usually ended at the same time as her credit. Her financial inclinations were shakier than ever. Even when she had money – after the sale of her old Paris apartment, or after receiving an advance on her memoirs from an American publisher – she spent it lavishly. More often than not, however, her bills went unpaid or else were covered by an admirer. Nevertheless, she was still as ready as ever to make the generous gesture. When, after Esenin's suicide, she inherited his estate of F.400,000,

amassed in royalties from the sale of his poetry in Russia, she refused to accept it. She believed that his peasant relatives needed the money more than she did.

She divided her time between Paris and Nice, where she rented a small theater in which she hoped eventually to start another school – this one to be financed by the pupils' parents. In Paris she negotiated with the Russian ambassador and the French Communist Party with a view to setting up a free school for the children of the people. Nothing was to come of either scheme. The only lasting fruit of the last years of her life was her autobiography, which she wrote to raise the money to pay her hotel bills.

She gave three performances in the spring of 1926 in Nice, and a final program at the Mogador in Paris in 1927. The friends and admirers who packed the halls found her dancing more static than in the past, but still imposing.

Yet, morally and physically, she was a shadow of her former self. Her appetite for life was as great as ever, but less of it went to the service of her art now that she rarely danced, and more into casual love affairs. She collected fresh admirers as other women collected calling-cards. The art critic Clive Bell first met her at this time in the studio of the painter Nils de Dardel. Balancing a large glass of brandy in one hand, she grabbed him with the other. As they collapsed together on to a sofa, she ran his hand over her body and proclaimed, "I am not a woman, I am a genius." She herself wrote in *My Life*, "Especially do I resent the conclusion formed by so many women that, after the age of forty, a dignified life should exclude all love-making. Ah, how wrong this is!"

She expected the admiration of attractive young men as hommage due to her although the men's wives were sometimes less than willing to concede this. On one occasion in the south of France, the Fitzgeralds found themselves eating in the same restaurant as her. Scott went over to introduce himself, sitting at her feet in her honor. Zelda stood the spectacle of Isadora flirting with him for some time, and then, without any warning, suddenly leapt over the table at which she had been sitting and down a flight of stairs into the darkness beyond. Scott found her bruised and shaken but otherwise unharmed, though the gesture could well have been fatal.

By this stage, Isadora was also drinking heavily. When James Joyce once mentioned to Robert McAlmon that he was considering sending his daughter to study with her sister Elizabeth because "Isadora isn't holding courses any more", McAlmon, who had seen her recently, replied "No, she isn't even holding her liquor."

Old age had never had a place in Isadora's life plan, so perhaps it was as well that she was spared its indignities. Her death, when it came in September, 1927, was hardly worthy of the romantic dreams of her youth, but had a Jazz Age quality about it that was apt enough for her later years. She was strangled when her red silk scarf got entwined in the wire wheels of a Bugatti sports car in which she was driving with a handsome young Niçois. Her friends later recalled her last, playful words as she drove off to her death: "*Adieu, mes amis. Je vais à la gloire!*"

Right: Isadora Duncan's melodramatic life ended in equally melodramatic tragedy.

7. The Rich are Very Different...

It was in the 1920s that the French first became convinced that all Americans were rich. They had seen wealthy individuals before, but nothing in their experience had prepared them for the cohorts of big spenders who flocked to their shores as the franc plummeted. By the time it stabilized at 25 to the dollar, it was worth only one-fifth of its prewar value against the American currency. At a time when French workers were taking home wages that averaged the equivalent of $9 a week, even median-income Americans appeared affluent. Maybe this view was exaggerated. Certainly the average American tourist was far from being the Croesus that Parisian shop and hotel owners imagined him to be. Yet by French standards most of the tourists *were* well off, and some were a good deal more than that. It was a time when spending came easily and nobody bothered to count the change.

By 1925 5,000 Americans were arriving in Paris each week. They came on the *Ile de France* and the *Leviathan*, the *Majestic* and the *Mauretania*, the *Berengaria* and the *Aquitania* – all those transatlantic pleasure-domes on which stenographers could set their sights on oil barons and at whose gangplanks Prohibition came to an end. For some passengers the voyage was a time for shuffleboard and skeet-shooting and brisk walks on deck. For others it was a week-long cocktail party culminating in wild last-night revels and instructions to the steward to "pour me ashore" at Cherbourg or Le Havre in the morning. The liners were alive with what Thomas Wolfe called "the life, the hate, the love, the bitterness, the jealousy, the intrigue of six-day worlds." Yet for all of their chandeliered luxury, they were only the prologue to the great adventure that began when the boat-trains reached their terminus in Paris.

For wealthy tourists, there began the round of cocktails at the Ritz, of dinners at La Pérouse, Voisin's, the Trianon, the Café de Paris, of shows at the Lido and the Casino de Paris, of onion soups in Les Halles bistros where tuxedoed carousers rubbed shoulders uneasily with meat porters at dawn. It was a time when every bartender spoke English, and the dollar fluttered triumphantly over the night clubs of Montmartre.

The daytime was for shopping, for as Lorelei Lee, the not-so-dumb heroine of *Gentlemen Prefer Blondes*, noted, shopping was what Paris really seemed to be principally for. It had been a center for luxury goods at least since the time of Louis XIV and Colbert, and the tradition had survived vigorously into the twentieth century. If the spiritual heart of Paris was the cathedral of Notre-Dame, its material heart beat somewhere in an area of the Right Bank bounded by the rue de Rivoli to the south, the *grands boulevards* to the

north, and to the east and west approximately by the avenue de l'Opéra and the rue Royale. Though for many wealthy visitors this opulent square mile included everything that they meant by 'Paris', in truth it belonged neither to the native Parisian nor to France but to the international confraternity of the rich. The God that was worshipped there was Mammon, and the principal rites centered on the ornamentation and beautification of the female form.

It was the district of *couturiers* and *parfumiers*, of jewellers, milliners and grand hotels. The sacred names were Lanvin and Lelong, Patou and Paquin, Coty, Cartier and Molyneux. By anyone's standards it was expensive. Within its confines some of the most spectacular French fortunes of the twenties were to be made. Yet in a way its expensiveness only increased its appeal. The prices that its clients were prepared to pay confirmed its status as a world center of luxury and elegance. The wives and daughters of the rich flocked to it as birds migrating to a homing-ground.

The shop owners of the Right Bank were not the only people to take advantage of the legendary riches of America. The aristocracy of France, which had had increasing difficulty in maintaining itself in the accustomed style throughout the nineteenth century, turned eagerly to the New World to redress the bank balances of the Old. It was the golden age of the American heiress. Boni de Castellane had set a trend before the war by marrying an extremely wealthy girl whose attractions certainly were not physical. There is a well-known story that, while showing guests around the marble-columned Pink Palace on the Avenue du Bois that was one of the fruits of his marriage, he dismissed the master bedroom with a rueful smile as "the penance chamber". After the two were divorced, he was quoted as saying "She will never know how much I loved her for her money."

Some of the heiresses put their money to good use. Winnaretta Singer, daughter of the sewing machine manufacturer, ran a famous musical salon after coming to Europe as the Princesse de Polignac where she held recitals of music commissioned from Stravinsky, Ravel, Milhaud and Falla. She was admired by Romaine Brooks, who painted her portrait. She fell into the highest category of wealth – that of the people who have no idea how much money they actually have. A story was told that once when she went to make a contribution to the Paris police welfare fund, she was snubbed by a desk officer who wanted to close the bureau; her reaction was to make out a check for ten million francs on the spot. Yet her wealth made her enemies as well as friends among the French aristocracy. Count Robert de Montesquiou, greatest of the Parisian dandies and the model for Proust's Baron Charlus, hated her. He once described her as looking like Nero, only more cruel – "one who dreamed of seeing her victims stitched up by sewing-machines".

Left: American tourists check their maps to identify famous sights from atop the Arc de Triomphe.

Above: Les Halles, the 'belly' of Paris.
Above right: Seafood restaurants, such as this one in Les Halles, specialized in snails.

French society, after the fashion of Boni de Castellane, tended to revenge itself for the wealth of its American parvenues by sneering at their lack of polish. A favorite butt of their jokes was Laura Corrigan. She was no heiress. Her story, in fact, had all the wondrous simplicity of a twentieth century fairy-tale. She was working as a telephone operator at a hotel in Cleveland, when one evening a guest rather the worse for drink asked her, sight unseen, to have dinner with him. He turned out to be lonely, exceedingly rich, and in poor physical condition. The next morning they got married but shortly afterwards he died. Left without ties and with a great deal of money, she set sail for Europe with the express intention of buying her way into European society, and in a sense she succeeded. The recipients of her largesse, however, had a great deal of fun at the expense of her naiveté. When she was about to set out on a tour of the East, someone asked her if she was going to see the Dardanelles; she replied, so it is said, that she had letters of introduction to them, but doubted if she would have the time to look them up. She once went to lunch at the Crosbys' apartment, bringing several dresses as a propitiatory offering. Harry Crosby, overcome by her name dropping during the course of the meal, asked her if she had met the Duchess of Malfi yet.

Like all good fairy-tales, however, her story had a happy ending. During the war, she not only sold her jewelry to help the French wounded, but also went to work in the hospitals. She won the soldiers' lasting gratitude, and became known in the French press as 'the American angel'.

However glittering and impressive it may have seemed to Laura Corrigan and her like, French society was in fact no longer as sure of itself as it had been in the past. Economically, the position of the great landed families of France had been steadily weakened, and only a handful of nobles retained the great houses and liveried retainers of former days. The *haut monde* of Marcel Proust was no more. Paris society in the twenties was to be made up of a growing number of self-made businessmen, *couturiers* and impresarios. It was a society that, more than ever before, was open to money and to talent.

The style of Parisian society had changed correspondingly. The formal brilliance of the dinners and receptions described by Proust had become *démodé*. Calling-cards, those *sine qua non* of nineteenth century polite society, were no longer much used except by elderly ladies. The new manner, pioneered before the First World War by men like Boni de Castellane and the *couturier* Paul Poiret, ran to originality and imagination, neither of them qualities for which the older aristocracy had been renowned. The unpardonable sin for the *tout Paris* of the twenties was to be boring. Diaghilev's admonition to Jean Cocteau, "Astonish me", became the password for a generation.

by people who can't afford them" – and Balfour was afterwards enticed into visiting a night club. He thanked her later for "the most delightful and degrading evening" he had ever spent.

She was an accomplished singer and pianist, and was soon in demand as a party entertainer, performing a repertoire that consisted mostly of then-unpublished Cole Porter songs given to her by the composer. At this stage she lived either with friends or in a succession of cheap, upper-storey rooms, and claimed to have a wardrobe of only two dresses. As her reputation grew, she was able to put her social talents to commercial use, first by opening two successive night clubs backed by the British-born *couturier* Edward Molyneux, and then by working as a press agent. Her first client was the dress designer Jean Patou, whom she persuaded to give free dresses to the wives of impoverished British aristocrats as publicity. She subsequently took on the cities of Venice, where she promoted the Lido, and of Monte Carlo, which had lost many of its wealthiest Russian and central European visitors in the upheavals that followed the First World War. Elsa set about enticing a fresh clientele of Americans and West Europeans by recommending the building of a new casino and a new luxury hotel with a swimming pool.

She found her real *métier*, however, in organizing parties and, more particularly, costume balls. She was by no means the only hostess in Paris with a taste for these. The costume ball was in its own way as typical of the twenties in France as *le jazz hot* and Negro revues. It was the point of contact between real life and the theater – and social life had rarely been so theatrical since the days of the court masques of Elizabethan Britain. Artists like Jean Cocteau and Christian Bérard were called upon to design costumes and decorations for such gatherings as the Pecci-Blunt's White Ball – Cocteau dressed his clients in white masks and wigs – and Baron de Gunzberg's *fête champêtre* in the Bois de Boulogne, for which Bérard transformed the Baron's town house into a vision of a farm by moving in painted wooden stage sets and wrapping all available surfaces in blue satin.

To the costume ball, Elsa added her own note of brashness and humor. Her fancy-dress parties were the wildest and most irresponsible of all. The 'Come As You Were' party she organized for the Méraud Guevaras was a classic of its kind. Guests were asked to come exactly as they were at the time their invitation was received, the invitations having been delivered by hand at odd hours of the day and night to ensure a certain diversity of apparel. To save the guests the embarrassment of travelling in taxis in their odd attire, charabancs with cocktail bars installed were hired to carry them to the party. An unintentional note of surrealism was added shortly after the guests arrived when all the lights fused.

Among the revellers were several ladies in slips, a couple of men wearing hairnets, and one *grande dame* with exactly half of her face made up. The Marquis de Polignac arrived in immaculate evening dress but without any trousers. However the evening's star turn was provided by Christian Bérard himself. He came in a dressing-gown, with the mouthpiece of a telephone attached to his right ear and with white make-up simulating shaving-cream lathered around his chin.

A young American woman who had no visible means of support and who was, in her own words, "fat and unattractive", was among those who saw most clearly the possibilities of the new situation. Elsa Maxwell arrived in Paris in 1919, when it was, as she noted avidly, "the scene of the peace negotiations and the center of forthcoming social acitivity". For the next ten years she relied entirely on her wits to keep her at the center of that acitivity, becoming one of the great party-givers and -goers in a decade of parties. "I brought to the rich a capacity for friendship and gaiety that offered escape from plush-lined boredom, casual sex without passion and excessive gambling without excitement," she noted in her autobiography. "I had imagination and they had money, a fair exchange of the commodity possessed by each side in greatest abundance."

She was above all else an opportunist. Her social career in Paris began with a chance meeting with Arthur Balfour, then Britain's Secretary of State for Foreign Affairs. On impulse she invited him to a dinner party at the Ritz, though at the time she had barely enough money of her own to tip the cloak-room attendant. Wealthier friends, eager for a chance to meet the statesman, bailed her out by paying for the dinner. At that stage she was such an *ingénue* that she had no idea what food to order, so she simply copied the menu from one of Boni de Castellane's most famous dinners – disregarding the fact that Boni was himself on the guest list. The dinner was of course a great success – one of Miss Maxwell's maxims was that "the best parties are given

Another memorable Elsa Maxwell innovation was the 'Scavenger Hunt'. At this party she offered a gallon jar of Patou perfume to the guest who brought back the most, or the most interesting, items in a given period of time from a list that included a slipper taken from Mistinguett on stage at the Casino de Paris; a black swan from the lake in the Bois de Boulogne; three hairs from the head of a red-headed woman; a work animal; a pompom from the beret of a French sailor; a chamber pot; and a monographed handkerchief from Baron Maurice de Rothschild's Paris home.

It was the kind of stunt that could only be staged once, and its results were predictably chaotic. Mistinguett was attacked on stage and had to finish her performance barefoot; her assailants escaped retribution because one happened to be a nephew of the Paris police chief. The black swan wounded two people. One guest provided a chamber pot surrealistically decorated with two painted eyes looking inquisitively out of it, and finally won the prize on the grounds of creativity. The greatest scandal was caused by Lady Mendl, the wife of a staff member of the British Embassy. She stole the cap of a sailor on guard duty outside the Ministère de la Marine. A note of protest was duly sent by the French authorities to the British government, and questions were later asked about the affair in the House of Commons.

The victims of Elsa Maxwell's pranks may not have been amused, but she did little harm to anything except their dignity. Living solely on high spirits and native shrewdness, she became a court jester to the bright young things of Paris, and her career was as much a monument to Paris in the twenties as that of her compatriot Josephine Baker.

Princes and parties were not, of course, the only attractions that drew wealthy Americans to Paris. There was also its status as a world capital of culture. Paris, like London and Florence, had long been a second home for rich American aesthetes, and it continued to be so in the postwar years. What did change was the character and style of the art lovers it attracted. Between the patrician survivors of the prewar intellectual colony and the wealthy bohemians of the twenties a very real generation gap developed.

Two stalwarts of the older generation were the novelist Edith Wharton and her lifelong friend, Walter van Rensselaer Berry, with whom she shared a town house in the rue de Varenne. Both were permanent expatriates and both were extremely wealthy. Berry was a successful international lawyer and was President of the American Chamber of Commerce in Paris. Edith Wharton was a best-selling authoress, whose books sold by the hundreds of thousands. In a good year she could expect to earn $75,000 from her writings, and yet royalties did not make up the bulk of her income. That came from inherited private means.

Above all they were cultivated. They were the last of the pure-bred Jamesians having known the great writer intimately as a friend. Mrs. Wharton was sufficiently proud of this attachment to hope that her final epitaph would be, "She was a friend of Henry James." Walter Berry had also been close to Marcel Proust, who had dedicated a book to

Left: Norma Norée, one of the stars of the Folies Bergere in 1925.

him. The world the couple mixed in after the war included the art critic Bernard Berenson, the poet Paul Valéry, and the more artistically minded members of the French aristocracy – the Comte and Comtesse de la Rochefoucauld, some of the Noailles, and the Duc de Gramont.

Their lives were structured and ceremonious: friends entertained to tea and conversation; formal dinners at the rue de Varenne, ending invariably with brandy and, for the men, cigars; a downstairs world of servants, who, even out of their masters' hearing, continued to address each other as Monsieur and Madame. Mrs. Wharton, in her entertaining, was a strict observer of the niceties of social behavior. She was formal even by the standards of the French aristocracy. "She is too organized," a duchess once complained. "One cannot even forget one's umbrella at Madame Wharton's with impunity."

The same neatness and refinement marked their private lives. Walter Berry occupied himself with his collection of paintings and his library, rich with such treasures as a first edition of de Quincey's *Opium Eater* and a leaf from the Gutenberg Bible. Mrs. Wharton, who spent less of her time in Paris after Berry's death in 1927, devoted the ten years of life that remained to her to writing, to the care of her small dogs, and to her great love, gardening of the two substantial rural properties – one an eighteenth century mansion to the north of Paris, the other a laicized Cistercian monastery near Hyères. By that time she and Gertrude Stein were the last survivors of the prewar generation of literary expatriates. But while Gertrude Stein's fame continued to grow, Mrs. Wharton retreated into solitude. As she herself noted, she seemed to the bright young things of the twenties like "a taffeta sofa under a gaslit chandelier".

The contrast between her cautious, ordered life and the waywardness of the younger generation was striking. At a time when shocking the elders was a matter of fashion, many of the postwar expatriates flung themselves into *la vie de bohème* with self-destructive abandon.

The prototype of the social rebel in Paris was the English-born Nancy Cunard. Her American mother, Lady Emerald Cunard, had, by marrying into the English nobility and by a natural flair for 'doing what is done' better than most people do it, made herself one of the arbiters of London society. Perhaps it was inevitable that, as a second-generation heiress, Nancy should react against her mother's example. In Paris she was soon renowned for her extravagant dress – she like to wear bone and ivory bracelets all the way up her arms – and for her wild parties. She mixed principally with writers and artists and wrote poetry, which she published (along with other writers' work) on her own small press. Her lovers included the French poet, Louis Aragon, and a black jazz musician called Henry Crowther. She smoked incessantly, drank heavily, and flirted with Communism. This was all too much for her mother, who complained bitterly of her ways. Nancy retaliated by writing and printing a venomous attack on her mother, which she despatched to all of the old lady's society friends.

The rebelliousness of the American heirs and heiresses of the Quarter was generally more muted. In the palmy days of the twenties there were plenty of children of wealthy parents who were only too happy to follow the art trail to Montparnasse, but the great majority of them were more

Below: The ladies of Maxim's have the obligatory bottle of champagne at teatime.
Left: Maxim's in the thirties had the best roast beef in Paris. Occasionally it had other diversions. Fridays were the best nights.

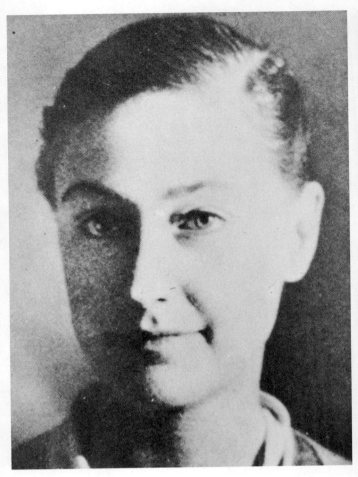

Above: Lady Duff Twysden and Harold Loeb, who became Lady Brett and Robert Cohen in Hemingway's *The Sun Also Rises*.

intent on maintaining good relations with their parents on whom they were financially dependent.

Two members of the Guggenheim clan featured prominently in the ranks of this bohemian plutocracy. One was Peggy Guggenheim, whose marriage to Lawrence Vail was the cause of much family concern. Vail, an artistic Jack-of-all-trades who dabbled in painting, sculpture and literature, was the Paris-born son of wealthy American parents. With his long blond hair and flaming red shirts, he was a noticeable figure even in Montparnasse, where he had something of a reputation in American circles as the King of the Bohemians. For seven years he and Peggy lived a migrant life in Europe. Vail had a temper to match his shirts, and his fighting instincts twice led him to jail, first on Capri and then in Paris. He was also once arrested for setting fire to a 100-franc note in the course of a café argument. Eventually he started fighting with his wife – he once tried to tear her clothes off in public – and they divorced. Vail subsequently involved himself with the novelist Kay Boyle, while Peggy Guggenheim entered an unsettled phase of her life that was to take her from Paris to London and back, and through a series of more of less unsatisfactory relationships. It was only in the late thirties that she found art collecting to be a satisfactory vocation.

Her cousin, Harold Loeb, was also in revolt against the family's financial traditions when he came to Europe in 1921. Loeb's rebellion was, however, an altogether more conscious and rationalized business. His interests were mainly literary. He founded and edited a little magazine called *Broom*, and was later to publish three novels. He was also to serve as the model for the unattractive figure of Robert Cohn in *The Sun Also Rises*. Hemingway had previously been a friend of Loeb's; the abrupt alteration in their relationship was due to their competition for the favors of Lady Duff Twysden – the Lady Brett Ashley of the book – who had left a baronet husband in England to escape to the bars of Montparnasse.

It is a long step from Edith Wharton's dinner parties to the emotional in-fighting of the Lost Generation, but both were a part of the experience of wealthy Americans in Paris in the twenties. On a few occasions the two worlds met face to face. One of these occurred when Scott Fitzgerald, who had long admired Edith Wharton's work, went to meet the ageing authoress at her chateau north of Paris. Nervous at the prospect of meeting her, he fortified himself with several drinks on the way. He found her surrounded by a polite circle of friends. He was in a combative mood, and broke into the conversation to demand (his own account):

"Mrs. Wharton, do you know what the matter with you is?"

"No. I've often wondered about that. Do tell me."

"You haven't had enough experience of life." He then sketched out some of the incidents of his life with Zelda in Europe, culminating with the disclosure that the hotel they

Above: The Gerald Murphys (left) and the Hemingways with bootblacks in 'the dangerous summer of 1926' in Pamplona.

had stayed in on first arriving in Paris had turned out to be a brothel.

He paused to enjoy the effect of this information on the old ladies. Mrs. Wharton gazed at him inquisitively. After a few moments' silence, she said encouragingly:

"But, Mr. Fitzgerald, you haven't told us what *happened* in the brothel."

Fitzgerald was vanquished. On the way back to Paris he kept repeating, "She beat me! She beat me!" It was a small moment of triumph and Mrs. Wharton no doubt savored it.

When Scott Fitzgerald wrote that "the very rich are different from you and me" he was not, of course, thinking merely of their money. He was thinking rather of a style of living that they have the means to afford but that is denied to other people. He was to discover in the course of his life that in fact very few wealthy people have the taste or the creativity to lead lives of the kind that he had imagined for them. However some artists were living the kind of life of which he approved, and among them were two American couples who lived in France in the twenties.

Gerald and Sara Murphy and Harry and Caresse Crosby had many things in common. All four were the children of wealthy families. Gerald Murphy's father was the founder and president of the Mark Cross leather-goods store in New York. Harry Crosby was a nephew of J. P. Morgan. The two wives had both been expensively educated, and had been debutantes in London. All four were also creatively minded and shared an interest in the contemporary arts.

Gerald, the eldest of the four, had been born in 1888; the youngest, Harry – he was six years younger than his wife – was born in 1898. The ten years made a great deal of difference in their two careers. Harry was only a youth of nineteen in 1917 when America entered the war, while Gerald, at 29, had already had time for a successful career at Yale, class of 1912, followed by five uncongenial years working in New York for his father's firm. It also partially explains a difference in their respective characters, Gerald's air of unshakeable assurance contrasting with Harry's occasional fits of boyish temperament.

Both couples made their way to Europe in 1921. At that time the Murphys had already been married for six years and had three children. Gerald had given up the idea of being a businessman, and for the past two years had been studying landscape architecture at Harvard. A trust fund that provided Sara with $7,000 a year had made the Murphys financially secure and free to travel. It was the passing of the Eighteenth Amendment that finally persuaded them to take the boat for France.

They were to remain in Europe for the next twelve years. The first three were spent mainly in Paris, where Gerald abandoned his earlier intention of pursuing a career in landscape gardening and turned his attention instead to painting. In the next nine years he finished ten canvases, exhibiting them in the Salon des Indépendents. Friends tended to regard his painting as at best a hobby – unjustly, for his work was both original and ahead of its time. He painted large still lifes, often of mechanical objects, in a bold, brash style that calls to mind the work of Stuart Davis and that led Fernand Léger to call Murphy "the only *American* painter in Paris". His work received ultimate recognition shortly before Murphy's death in 1964, when a retrospective exhibition of his work was staged and when one of his canvases was accepted by the New York Museum of Modern Art.

Below: Una, Lady Troubridge, as drawn in 1924 by her friend Romaine Brooks.

Below : Two scenes of the fancy dress and undress at the Nice Carnival in 1931.

23

Left and above: Two fancy dress balls, one in Paris in 1925 (left) and the Côte d'Azur in 1931. Fancy dress parties were popular throughout the interwar period.

Yet, faced with W. B. Yeats's choice between "perfection of the life or of the work", the Murphys ultimately settled for living. They gave the first of the parties for which they were to become famous on board a barge in the Seine in 1923. The occasion was the opening of Diaghilev's Russian Ballet production of Stravinsky's *Les Noces*. The guest list included the composer and the producer, as well as such notables of Parisian artistic society as Picasso, Jean Cocteau, the composer Darius Milhaud, the conductor Ernst Ansermet, and the writers Tristan Tzara and Blaise Cendrars. It was the sort of gathering that could have taken place nowhere else in the world, and at no other time than the 1920s. In the course of the evening Cocteau, turned out in a full captain's uniform, was to be seen wandering from room to room carrying a lantern and announcing mournfully "We're sinking". Even Stravinsky grew light-hearted enough to take a running jump through a massive laurel wreath rescued from the decorations by his secretary and Ernst Ansermet. Picasso made sculptures with the children's toys the Murphys had bought to decorate the dinner tables. The party earned a place for itself in the footnotes of Parisian social history, and was probably the most memorable thrown by any American anywhere during the entire decade.

Yet the Murphy's name is now remembered less often in connection with Paris than with the Riviera, whose popu-

larity as a summer resort they helped to pioneer. In the early twenties the hot midsummer months were regarded very much as the off-season on the Côte d'Azur. Virtually all visitors left by the end of May, and through June, July and August the hotels closed down, It was Cole Porter, whom Gerald knew from Yale, who first drew the Murphys' attention to the possibilities of the deserted coast. In 1922 they spent a couple of weeks with him in a villa he had rented at Cap d'Antibes. The following year they persuaded the owner of the Hôtel du Cap to keep the place open, with a minimal staff. They had cleared one corner of a small beach, la Garoupe, of seaweed the previous summer, and they returned there to swim and sunbathe. They also received the first of the many guests whom they were to invite to Antibes, among them Picasso, who came with his wife, Olga, and his mother. By the end of the summer they were sufficiently convinced of the success of their experiment to have decided to buy a villa of their own. Before returning to Paris they had found and christened the Villa America, which for the next decade was to be their principal home.

The full story of their life at the villa has been told in Calvin Tomkins' best-selling biography, named from the Spanish motto which they adopted: *Living Well is the Best Revenge*. It was there that they entertained the Hemingways, John and Katy Dos Passos, Fernand Léger, the Benchleys, Dorothy Parker, Archibald MacLeish and his wife. It was also there that Scott Fitzgerald, the most charming but also the most difficult of guests, conceived the idea of *Tender is the Night*. Almost single-handedly they turned Antibes from

Below: The carnival procession passes through the streets of Nice.
Right: A bathing beauty of 1928 on the Côte d'Azur.

Above: Preparing for a Sunday ride in the Bois de Boulogne.

a quiet provincial village, where the telephone service only operated in working hours and where the cinema opened one night a week, into an internationally known resort. Like others who have had similar experiences elsewhere, they lived to regret their own success; the exclusive, crowded and snobbish Antibes of 1934 seemed to have little relation to the tranquil village that they had once known.

Originally, they chose the villa for its garden. It was planted with exotic trees and shrubs that the previous owner, a French army officer, had brought back from his travels in the Near East. There were date palms, pepper trees, lemon trees, Arabian maples. Above all, there was a view across the bay to Cannes and, in the distance, the mountains of the Esterel. The Murphys added a second storey and a sun-roof to the one-storey building. There were also two cottages in the grounds, one of which Gerald used as a studio; the other helped to house their many guests. In addition, they retained a small apartment in Paris which they visited at least once a month to keep in touch with the capital's artistic and social life.

They developed a style of living at the Villa America that managed to be both informal and carefully planned at the same time. Though normally a careful dresser (he had been voted best-dressed man of his class at Yale), Gerald contented himself on the coast with striped matelot jerseys and white duck pants, setting a style that was soon popular along the entire coast. The furnishings of the villa were also tastefully simple, consisting mainly of plain wood tables – their legs painted black – and wickerwork café chairs. Guests could listen to their choice of the latest records, both jazz and classical, which Gerald and Sara imported directly from America. Sara's cuisine was eclectic, including favorite American recipes alongside the Provençal dishes of the region.

One ingredient that contributed to the special flavor of a visit to the Villa America was the presence of the Murphys' three children, Honoria, Baoth and Patrick. They formed an integral part of the household, and some guests went to great lengths to keep them amused. Scott Fitzgerald once spent a whole day inventing an elaborate medieval game for them, complete with an enormous sand-castle, tin soldiers provided by Gerald Murphy, and a black beetle to serve as a dragon. Another time the Murphys themselves provided the entertainment. They took the children to a deserted cove near St. Tropez, where without their knowledge they had previously buried an antique-looking treasure map. They took great pains to ensure that its discovery appeared to be a matter of chance. The map led, through a series of clues, to a buried sea-chest filled with old compasses, spyglasses and jewelry – all of which Gerald and Sara had previously bought in antique shops, though they never let the children know.

The guests were sometimes more difficult to please – especially Scott Fitzgerald when he was in his cups. At one of the Murphy's parties he threw an olive at the bare back of the Princesse de Caraman-Chimay, a total stranger to him who was conversing with friends across the room. The princess stiffened, but otherwise made no reaction. Archibald MacLeish took him aside to remonstrate with

Above: A performance of Halevy's *Ballet de la Juive* in the Bois de Boulogne.

him, and was rewarded for his interference with a right to the jaw. After that incident, Scott was formally banished from the Villa America for three weeks. He respected the sentence, and reappeared with Zelda, charming as ever, on the morning of the twenty-second day.

The exploits of Scott and Zelda on the Riviera became almost legendary. On one occasion Zelda rose from her table at the Casino at Juan-les-Pins and, to the astonishment of the entire room, began to dance, alone, on the empty floor. With the aid of friends, she and Scott once kidnapped the owner and waiters of a small Cannes bistro. They released them only after having scared them half out of their wits with threats to saw them in two. Another evening, returning home from a dinner with the Murphys in Saint-Paul-de-Vence, Scott took a wrong turning and managed to jam his car on a street-car trestle. Unconcernedly the two proceeded to fall asleep. They were wakened and rescued the following morning by a passing farmer just half an hour before the first trolley of the day was due to arrive.

Mercifully unaffected by the Fitzgeralds' vagaries, the Murphys continued to live a happy and tranquil life. The pleasant monotony of days in the sun was broken from time to time by trips to Paris and by other voyages – to Schruns and skiing with Dos Passos and his wife, to Pamplona for the fiesta with Ernest and Pauline Hemingway, to central Europe with the MacLeishes. There were also sea voyages on the 100-foot schooner they had built to the specifications

of a Russian friend who had designed sets for Diaghilev. They christened the boat the *Weatherbird*, a name chosen from the title of a Louis Armstrong record that they had sealed into the helm for luck.

The peace of the Villa America was first seriously troubled in 1929. For the Murphys it was not the Crash but their children who were unwittingly to prove the weak link in the chain of contentment around which they had built their lives. Their younger son, Patrick, developed tuberculosis and was sent to a sanatorium in the Swiss Alps. The whole family moved there to keep him company, and set about trying to recreate something of the Villa America atmosphere in the less promising environment of a mountain health resort. They were to return to Antibes in 1931 when Patrick's health seemed much improved, and spent another two years there. But in 1933, when his symptoms recurred, they decided to take him back to America. The *Weatherbird* was sold, and the villa closed down.

They were never to return to it. In the course of the thirties they lost not merely Patrick, but Baoth also. Gerald was obliged to take charge of the ailing family business, a task he carried out for the rest of his working life with success but with little real interest or pleasure. In New York, Sara and he continued to keep in touch with their friends and to lead pleasingly civilized lives, but they were never to recapture the carefree gaiety of the days in the Villa America.

Harry Crosby's life was also crossed by tragedy in the fateful year of 1929 though in his case it was self-inflicted. Although he fully shared the Murphys' concern with living well, there had long been a morbid streak in his tempera-

Right and below: Almost as popular as the Côte d'Azur for Parisians if not most Americans were the beaches of Normandy, where the occasionally icy winds from the Channel were balanced by the Casinos at Deauville and Trouville and their proximity to the capital. Building sand castles was as popular in western France as it was on the North Sea coast in resorts such as Scheveningen and Ostend.

Above: A restaurant on the Champs Elysées which had a special menu for canine gourmets.
Right: A party for Russian royalty at Josephine Baker's in 1927.
Below right: Elegant party for Parisian *haut-monde*.

ment that led him towards excess. He never possessed the Murphys' sense of moderation and balance. There was a wildness about him that led him to pack the experiences of several ordinary lives into a single decade. It was as if he had known from the start the needlessly early death that lay in store for him.

All of that was a long way away in 1921 when he brought his bride, then plain Polly Crosby, to Paris, where he worked for his uncle's bank. Polly's name was not to be changed to Caresse until several years later, when the two were about to publish their first joint book of poetry. Finding the signature 'Harry and Polly Crosby' insufficiently poetic, they decided to rechristen her. They chose the name Caresse because it sounded euphonious, then went along to the local *mairie* to make it official.

At the time of their first meeting in 1919, Harry had been 21, and was studying at Harvard. Polly was in the last stages of an unhappy first marriage that had foundered on her husband's alcoholism. The divorce was finalized two years later. Harry at once launched into a tempestuous courtship of the divorcée, flying her to Venice where the two of them registered at a hotel as the Count and Countess Myopia. Caresse soon fled back to New York and respectability, but soon afterwards Harry flew over from Paris, his home at that time, to persuade her to marry him at once. They were wed on the day of his arrival, enabling him to collect on a $100 bet he had made with a friend.

He was less eager to take on his wife's two children, whom he resented. They were sent away to boarding schools, and for the next few years their mother had to steal time away from her husband to keep in touch with them even in a sporadic manner.

Their life together was unconventional from the start. Harry was working for his uncle's bank near the Place de la Concorde. Like any young businessman he commuted to work each morning – only he travelled by canoe. Caresse and he would row up from the Ile St. Louis, where they then lived, to the Pont de la Concorde; Harry would disembark, leaving Caresse to paddle home alone. Though the Crosbys were well-connected (Walter Berry was a cousin of Harry's), they had little respect for social conventions. They once startled the guests at a tea-party given by Count Etienne de Beaumont by bringing their whippet, Narcisse, decked out with a gold necklace and with gold-lacquered toenails.

Harry Crosby was extravagant in all things, including his generosity. Presents for servants were always bought new from good shops; he made a rule against handing on cast-off possessions. For the street flower-seller from whom he nightly bought a bouquet for his wife, he provided a folding camp-stool imported specially from England, and a daily cup of coffee on account at a local bistro.

Occasionally he could be reckless. Once when he and

Below: The Bal des Loufoques in Montmartre.

Caresse had decided it was unwise to keep her uninsured jewelry in their apartment, he scooped her pearl necklaces, diamond bracelets and ruby and sapphire bar-pins into a Cartier bag and set off by taxi to deposit them in a bank-vault. As the cab turned into the rue Castiglione, Harry noticed his cousin walking down the street. He leapt out of the cab, telling the driver to wait, while he and his cousin disappeared into a nearby bar. He returned several porto flips later, and was genuinely surprised to find the cab, its driver and the jewelry all gone without trace.

The Crosbys had a busy social life. Their friends formed an interesting cross-section of Parisian society, ranging from aesthetes like Walter Berry, who left the bulk of his library to the couple, to the curiously-named Goops, a petty gangster who had been Harry's batman in the Ambulance Corps during the War. In a bar one day, Harry jokingly complained about an unwanted wealthy relative. The faithful Goops at once offered to liquidate the offender for $100, which Harry – never one to flunk a gesture – promptly handed over to him. Nothing more came of it, except that Simenon, who had been with them in the bar, borrowed the situation as the starting-point of his novel, *La Tête d'un Homme*.

The couple were always eager to make new friends. Among their acquaintances was a group of architecture students, who repaid their hospitality by inviting them to the famous Quatz' Arts Ball. These licensed bacchanalia of Parisian art students were for many years the highlight of

the city's bohemian life. The Crosby's contribution was
extravagant even on the Ball's permissive terms. After providing a champagne supper for the entire class, they set off
on a triumphal procession up the Champs Elysées, in which
Caresse rode on a baby elephant hired for the occasion from
an agency, while the future Earl of Portsmouth, a friend of
the Crosbys, pranced ahead of her waving a spear.

Inside the ballroom, Caresse, naked to the waist and
wearing a long blue wig, was the principal ornament of the
students' dragon float. Harry wore a collar of dead pigeons,
and carried a bagful of live snakes.

The night ended as riotously as it had begun. Caresse,
accompanied by one of the more attractive young male
students, returned home to find her husband sharing their
sunken marble bath with three pretty girls. Their bed held
seven people that night – the seventh being a total stranger
who found his way to the bedroom dressed only in a loin-
cloth and who disappeared equally mysteriously the next
morning muttering that he had to attend a class.

The bedroom in the large and aristocratic mansion
behind the Gare d'Orsay that became their final Paris home
played an unusually important part in their lives. Besides
sleeping in bed, Harry liked to entertain there. Promptly at
eight o'clock each evening, Caresse and he would undress
and get beneath the sheets. Guests were then invited in to
sit at small tables around the bedside. Harry would sometimes invite them to avail themselves of the luxurious bathroom, with its white bearskin rug and open fireplace. The

Above: A revealing night club near the Moulin Rouge.
Below: The Tribune des Dames or 'ladies stand' at
Chantilly race course in 1936.

Above: Wealthy riders on the Avenue Foch head for an outing in the Bois de Boulogne. Sunday was the best day for a ride in the park.
Right: A young man of fashion.

night of the Quatz' Arts Ball was by no means the only time that the tub held four people.

The Crosbys found their equivalent of the Villa America nearer to Paris. It was an old mill on the Ermenonville estate of their friend Count Armand de la Rochefoucauld. It was empty when the Crosbys first saw it, and they decided at once that they wanted to buy it. Harry impulsively asked the Count how much he wanted for it. He demurred at setting a figure. Harry, always a gambler, offered to make out a check for the balance of his bank account, specifying that it was somewhere between F.40,000 and F.400,000 – he wasn't sure of the exact figure. The Count accepted the gamble, and Harry, for want of a check book, scribbled out instructions to his bank on the cuff of Caresse's dress, which he tore off and handed to his friend. It was duly presented and accepted by Harry's bank, and the sum turned out to be, from the Count's point of view, very satisfactory.

In the same year – 1927 – Harry finally gave up his job at the bank to devote himself to literature. Caresse and he had private incomes that were quite sufficient to support them, even in relative luxury. They had also recently found a printer to handle the books they intended to publish. Under the imprint of the Black Sun Press, they were to bring out short texts by several important writers, including James Joyce and D. H. Lawrence. They also printed the first, de luxe edition of Hart Crane's *The Bridge*. They had

played a part in the creation of this work, for when Crane was having difficulty finishing it they had him shut up at the Mill, where he could work without fear of interruption and was provided with regular meals and a crate of Cutty Sark, until the poem was completed.

Their publishing ventures often had a quixotic air about them. Harry paid Lawrence for his manuscript *Sun* with twenty twenty-dollar gold pieces. Needing to convey the gold quickly to him in Italy, he wrapped it in a package and went to the Gare de l'Est to search the Florence train for a suitable courier. Just before the train pulled out, he noticed an aristocratic looking man leaning out of a window. Handing him the package, Harry asked if he would be so kind as to post it on his arrival in Florence. Surprisingly enough the stranger agreed. He merely asked, half-jokingly, if there was a bomb inside. Crosby assured him that, on the contrary, it contained gold for a poet. Amazingly enough the package did reach Lawrence. It was delivered by hand by the gentleman, who turned out to be the Duke of Argyll.

For the remaining two years of his life Harry delved deeply into the morbid world of his own poetry. He had been obsessed with death at least since 1918, when he had had a near encounter with it as an ambulance driver exposed to prolonged German bombardment in a stalled column outside Verdun. At first his death-wish was balanced by a life-oriented cult of sun worship that he sometimes carried to bizarre lengths. Once on a trip to Egypt, he had gone to illicit tatooists to have the sun mark etched permanently on his back, and had suffered all the agonies of hell at their hands, strapped half-naked to the bottom of a boat on the Nile while a lecherous old bedouin made advances on Caresse under his helpless gaze. However

the two dominant images of his imagination soon fused into a single idea, that of the sun-death.

This mystical concept of glorious annihilation was rarely far from his thoughts. In 1929 he learned to fly, apparently with the half-formed idea of an aerial suicide in mind. He often spoke of the sun-death to Caresse, and even persuaded her to join him in a suicide compact by which both were to undergo it together. But she was too cheerful and content a person to take his obsession seriously. For her the planned sun-death was simply one of the private games with which her odd but lovable husband enlivened their marriage.

In December, 1929, the Crosbys returned to New York for a short visit, to look up relatives and to see the Yale-Harvard football game. They stayed at the Savoy-Plaza in New York, and took the opportunity to renew contact with some old friends, including Hart Crane who threw a party for them a few days before they were due to return to France. At the party, Harry seemed pensive but in good spirits. The following day he left Caresse at lunchtime. He was expected to join her again for tea with his mother and his uncle, J. P. Morgan. He failed to turn up. When he also failed to meet a dinner engagement with Hart Crane, Caresse began to worry. She called an artist friend whose apartment Harry sometimes borrowed.

They found him in the studio shortly afterwards. He was not alone. With him was a wealthy and attractive young married woman called Josephine Rotch Bigelow who had for some time been his mistress. Both were dead, shot through the head with a pistol. They had been drinking Scotch. There was no sign of panic or of a struggle. On the contrary, the evidence suggested that Mrs. Bigelow had proved a willing accomplice in the deed. Harry Crosby had died as he had lived, comfortably, extravagantly, and apparently in the best of spirits.

Below: Members of the Diplomatic Corps and the Académie Française arrive for a night at the opera.

Right: A wealthy holidaymaker at her ease on the beach at Deauville.
Below: The Grand Restaurant and the beach at Nice.

8. After the Crash

The French heard the news of the Crash of 1929 with awed but distant curiosity. The panic selling that was to wipe out fifty billion dollars' worth of paper profits in a matter of weeks, the bankruptcies, the suicides: seen from a distance they all seemed very much a transatlantic phenomenon, a Jazz Age extravaganza turned sour. The Crash was disconcerting, it was tragic, and it was foreign. France was finally returning to prosperity, and Wall Street seemed a long way away.

A few Frenchmen were more directly concerned. They were those who had invested their savings in American stocks. Among them was the family of Maurice Sachs, which lost its entire fortune. Sachs's mother had a heart attack on learning the news; an uncle committed suicide. Sachs himself was thrown back on his wits. He survived the next decade by bolstering his meager literary earnings with the profits of shady art and antique dealing, only to die in a Nazi concentration camp during the war – apparently killed by fellow-inmates who suspected him of being an informer. By a cruel irony of fate the chronicler of the *années folles* was one of the first victims of its passing.

For the majority of Frenchmen, 1929 and 1930 were years of affluence. The country's economy seemed healthy. War reconstruction work was finally completed; the franc was steady; unemployment was almost non-existent; production was booming; and salaries were up by a third on prewar levels. The Paris social world had never been gayer or more extravagant. The *tout Paris* amused themselves at parties and balls like that given by the *couturier* Jean Patou, who wrapped his house and garden down to the twigs on the trees in silver foil, imported the baritone Whispering Jack Smith as an entertainer, and raffled off lion cubs as presents for his guests.

The only real change noticeable in Paris was the sudden decline in the number of American visitors. The year, 1929 had been a boom year for tourists, in quantity if not in quality. The old Paris hands of the American community had been overwhelmed. Scott Fitzgerald wrote vindictively of the newcomers of that year as "fantastic neanderthals who believed something, something vague, that you remembered from a very cheap novel." By 1930 the hordes were no longer coming.

The loss of the tourist dollars was the first real blow that the French economy suffered. The Parisian luxury trades were the hardest hit. In the Faubourg St. Honoré the dressmakers were reciving fewer customers and the jewellers of the rue de la Paix were plagued with cancelled orders. The flourishing trade in reproduction antiques

Left: The rue St Julien-le-Pauvre near Notre Dame in 1933. The shadows of the 1930s grew longer as the slump took its toll.

received a body blow, and the great hotels were left with empty rooms to fill. American business at the Ritz fell off so sharply that its manager had to stoop to the economy of buying his foodstuffs directly from the markets, rather than through the hotel's traditional suppliers. Charles Ritz went in person to America to drum up business, coining a slogan for hard times: "The Ritz is not ritzy".

Café and night club owners also found their receipts lowered, and the big stores and souvenir shops discovered that their "English spoken here" signs were netting fewer customers. Proprietors soon began to miss the sound of American voices. That was nothing new, though. Henry James had noted during the exodus following the American financial crisis of 1873 that "the American idiom is dear to Parisian ears, and the sorrows of Wall Street find an echo on the boulevards."

It took quite some time before the echo was heard in other parts of France. In the twenties, business and political leaders had complained about the country's slow industrial progress, but paradoxically it was the lack of industrialization that was to protect France from the worst effects of the Slump. In 1930, France was still a country of peasants and small businesses; even though the index of industrial production was 38 percent up on prewar levels, 60 percent of all France's workers still worked for firms employing less than twenty people. It was the few big enterprises whose successes had been the wonder of the twenties that were the first to suffer from the new economic conditions. André Citroën went bankrupt, while the small businesses of France, like the tortoise in the fable, kept on going. Because of their survival, the country's economy was protected from sudden total collapse. In France the Depression arrived in slow motion.

But come it did. By 1932 the unemployment figures had risen to 300,000 – very few compared with America's ten million unemployed, but large by French standards – and the country's economic and political problems were deepening. Less than a year after the 1931 elections, France's new President – a mild-mannered Auvergnat called Doumer without a known enemy in the world -- was assassinated by a crazed Russian. In the course of the next two years, the social peace was further shaken by a series of scandals which culminated with the multiple frauds perpetrated by a petty con-man turned international financier by the name of Alexandre Stavisky. Stavisky's swindles involved some 18 million dollars, several deputies and a few cabinet ministers.

The agitation aroused by the Stavisky affair was to climax in the riots of February 6, 1934 – 'Bloody Tuesday'. Mobs of French Rightists, mixed with contingents from veterans' associations and with a smaller number of opportunistic Communists, laid siege to the National Assembly. After an evening of fighting, during which some 2,000 rounds of

Right: A French housewife peels potatoes in her kitchen.
Above: Nine workers who demolished an old house in
the rue Mouffetard discovered $70,000 in gold pieces in
1938, part of the fortune of Louis Nivelle, Equerry to
Louis XV. They celebrate here after finding an additional
$20,000 in gold and silver pieces in a few small sacks.

small-arms ammunition were fired into the crowd, the Parisian police had managed to keep control of the Pont de la Concorde which alone stood between the demonstrators, gathered in the Place de la Concorde, and the French parliament building. The cost in human lives was variously reckoned as between twenty and seventy. Order was restored and the republic was saved, but France was no longer the carefree and prosperous nation it had been at the turn of the decade. The *années folles* had passed, to be succeeded by the *années difficiles*.

The fate of American residents in France in the troubled days of the early thirties depended largely on the source of their incomes. The Crash had immediately weeded out most of the hangers-on, who depended on the charity of parents or friends. In the twenties, as Scott Fitzgerald put it, "even when you were broke you didn't worry about money, because it was in such profusion around you." In the thirties there was less loose cash around, and those who had depended on checks from home usually took the boat back to America.

Americans with homes in France suffered heavy personal losses during the Crash, and had either to cut down on or to give up their French establishments to make the necessary economies. 'Château for sale' notices began to appear frequently in the property columns of France's English-language newspapers. The singer Mary Garden was doubly unfortunate: not only did she have to sell her villa at Beaulieu-sur-Mer to cover her debts, but also lost most of her jewelry. Like Harry Crosby, she left her jewelry bag by accident in a taxi cab; also like the Crosbys, she had not insured the gems.

The shock waves set in motion by the Crash were eventually to affect most of the American businesses in France, and especially those that depended mainly on visiting Americans. The *Chicago Tribune's* Paris edition closed down putting many Paris-based newspapermen out of work. Business was so slow at Shakespeare and Company that Sylvia Beach had to consider closing the bookstore. It was only saved by the efforts of her friends.

Those least affected by the Depression were the wealthy expatriates whose private means had not been reduced by the collapse of the stock market, and those Americans in France who in one way or another earned their money from the French. The first group included Natalie Barney and Gertrude Stein for whom the thirties were a time of literary and financial success. There was also Caresse Crosby, who returned to France after the suicide of her husband. She continued publishing books and through her *Crosby Continental Editions* even made a pioneering venture into the paperback publication of modern classics. She also continued to entertain lavishly at the Mill. For one of her costume balls, the Polignac family provided her with eighty magnums of its own champagne, Pommery Nature. In the thirties, however, the guests were almost all French. The American 'wild crowd' she and Harry had mixed with had, for the most part, gone home.

The other category included figures as disparate as Man Ray and Josephine Baker. Both careers were prospering.

Left: A working class suburban alley on the outskirts of Paris in 1933, when the Depression began to bite.

Above: A cobbled street in Menilmontant down the northern slope of Montmartre in 1930.

Ray could afford the luxury, not only of a fast car, but also of a *residence secondaire* in St. Germain-en-Laye. As for Josephine Baker, she reached new heights of prestige in 1935 when she was invited to perform in a charity gala at the Opera before the President of France. The following year she returned to America for a less than triumphant engagement with the Ziegfeld Follies, but by 1937 she was back in Paris with a cabaret of her own in the rue François Ier and a new show at the Folies Bergère. Only an unsuccessful first marriage and the loss of a baby in childbirth were to mar the last years of a generally happy decade for her.

The Paris that she knew and represented was hardly touched by the Depression. The city's nightlife was as brilliant as ever. It takes more than political unrest and economic uncertainty to prevent Parisians from enjoying themselves, and in some respects *la vie parisienne* was even more splendidly animated in the thirties than at the height of the *années folles*. Nineteen thirty-seven, for instance, was the year of the Great Exhibition, to which Paris still owes such monuments as the Palais de Chaillot, the Palais de la Découverte, the Musée de l'Homme and the Musée d'Art Moderne. In the following year the Surrealists had their own complete exhibition at the Galérie des Beaux Arts. It included such original touches as recordings of hysterical laughter for background noises, and an opening-night reception without any lighting – the guests were provided with flashlights with which to examine the works.

Paris had preserved its gaiety and originality, but its position in the world had altered nonetheless. It was no longer the focus for all eyes that it had been in the twenties. Foreigners still regarded it as a wonder among cities, but they no longer considered it as the Capital of Mankind.

It was not Paris but the world that had changed. The issues that concerned people in 1935 were tragic. In an

Above: Workers repave a Parisian street in 1932. Most people kept their jobs in the thirties, but pay, particularly in dollar terms, was abysmally low.

Above: Wallis Warfield Simpson and the Duke of Windsor on their wedding day in 1937.
Right: The Duke and Duchess of Windsor returning to the Gare de l'Est after a trip to Austria in 1937.

atmosphere of gathering misery, hatred and war, the Parisian preoccupation with pleasure seemed frivolous and petty. The expatriates who thronged the café terraces of Montparnasse were no longer Americans looking for art and life, but German refugees fleeing Nazi persecution. By 1936 Spain was the place on which the attention of writers and artists was centered. Paris became, for Hemingway and others, merely a pleasant place in which to relax en route to or from the serious business of the Spanish civil war.

Perhaps it was the prevailing seriousness of purpose that gave such a feeling of unreality to the Anglo-American press's greatest French news story of the decade. The flight of Mrs. Wallis Simpson to France, and her subsequent marriage there to the Duke of Windsor, who but for the marriage, would still have been King Edward VIII of England, attracted international headlines, but seemed to have as little to do with the grim facts of life in 1937 as the wedding of Cinderella. The marriage of an ex-King to the twice-divorced socialite from Baltimore made for a story that was part fairy-tale, part tragedy, and part sentimental novel. In Britain, it was also serious politics. The abdication crisis split the country and threatened the stability of Prime Minister Stanley Baldwin's government. But the French elements in the story belonged to the purest tradition of theatrical farce.

Edward had first met the Simpsons in 1931. By the time that he had became King, in January 1936, the marriage was breaking up and he and Wallis were in love. They made little attempt to hide their relationship. Wallis accompanied the King on a well-publicized summer tour of the Mediterranean, and by the time that her divorce petition was heard in the provincial remoteness of Ipswich in October, she was headline news in the American and French press. But not in Britain. British editors, though fully aware of the story, followed a policy of discretion. Her name was not even mentioned in British newspapers.

The story was, after all, a difficult one to handle. How could any newspaper explain that the King of England was apparently considering marriage to a woman who was not merely a commoner but also twice divorced? As titular head of the Church of England, the King was expected to represent an institution that did not officially recognize divorce. The situation was *de facto* absurd. In the illusory calm of press self-censorship, the King was granted time to reconsider.

Rumors nonetheless were circulating, and Prime Minister Baldwin, in his role as advisor and counsellor to the monarch, finally took it upon himself to broach the question of the King's intentions. The two soon found that their positions on the issue were irreconcilable. Edward intended to marry Mrs. Simpson. Baldwin insisted that the marriage was impossible.

Once the British government started to concern itself with the situation, the newspapers' policy of silence quickly became untenable. It was the knowledge that the long-delayed press storm was about to break about her head that finally drove Mrs. Simpson across the Channel. She made arrangements to stay with American friends of hers, Mr. and Mrs. Herman Rogers, in their villa near Cannes.

The journey to France was planned amid an atmosphere of intrigue worthy of a Dumas novel. Edward asked Lord Brownlow, one of his Lords-in-Waiting and a personal friend, to accompany Mrs. Simpson. Tickets were reserved for the couple, under assumed names, on the Newhaven-Dieppe night ferry. Everyone concerned with the undertaking was pledged to absolute secrecy.

They set off for Newhaven in Lord Brownlow's Rolls-Royce; Mrs. Simpson's own car had been booked on to the ferry in advance. Their first problem arose when the car was stopped by police for speeding; only the presence of a detective bodyguard saved them from disclosure. No further incidents marred the journey to France, but as soon as they reached Dieppe, the storm broke.

Mrs. Simpson's car had, by some ludicrous oversight, been registered in her own name. She was recognized by the French customs officials, and from that moment the news of her presence in France was out. The journey to Cannes became a tragi-comic sequence of alarms and excursions as the luckless couple did their best to evade the crack troops of the French press. Mishaps lined their route south. There was a long-distance telephone call to Edward in England rendered inaudible by a bad connection. The key to Wallis's secret code of communication with the King was left by error in a Normandy inn. In a hotel in Rouen, an actress from the Comédie Française recognized Mrs. Simpson and gathered a crowd with her cry of "*Voilà la dame!*" By the time the two reached the Rogers' villa, their trip had become the worst-kept secret in Europe and a small army of French pressmen were waiting outside to greet them.

Above: Britain's former king and his consort decided to live permanently in Paris in 1938.

Above: The Duke and Duchess at the Palace of Versailles in 1938.

Mrs. Simpson remained at the villa throughout the six months required for her divorce to become absolute. During that time the King was to discover that the English Establishment, as personified by Stanley Baldwin's cabinet, was not prepared to consider the idea of accepting a divorcée even as a morganatic wife for their King, let alone as Queen of England. Presented with the choice of provoking a major constitutional crisis, renouncing Mrs. Simpson, or abdicating from the throne, he chose to abdicate.

Even then the couple's troubles were not over. They had to live apart until Mrs. Simpson's divorce became absolute. When finally reunited, they were faced with the problem of deciding where and how their marriage should be solemnized. There was no question of their returning to England, so they were thrown back on the hospitality of numerous sympathizers who offered the use of their homes in France. One offer came from Gerald Murphy, who offered them the use of the Villa America.

The choice they finally made could, in retrospect, hardly have been worse. They settled for a chateau owned by one Charles Eugene Bedaux, a French national who had made a fortune as the owner of a string of management-consultancy agencies in the United States. Bedaux was already known for his extreme Right Wing political views, and was ultimately to commit suicide in a French prison cell while awaiting trial for collaboration with the Germans during the Second World War. His influence on the couple was disastrous. In particular, he encouraged the Duke to make a well-publicized tour of Nazi Germany that lost him much of the popular support that he had earlier won.

Given a place in which to get married, the couple still had to find someone to marry them. The Duke wanted an Anglican ceremony, but the Church of England was opposed to the marriage. There was no possibility of an officially sanctioned wedding. They had eventually to accept the services of a rebel vicar, from the northern town of Darlington, who came to France against the specific instructions of his bishop to perform the ceremony.

So it came about that the most discussed marriage of the twentieth century was finally solemnized by a recalcitrant clergyman in the home of a future collaborationist. Shortly after the ceremony the Duke and Duchess set off, with 266 separate pieces of baggage, on their long-delayed honeymoon. It was a muted kind of happy ending for the love story of the decade.

In the thirties, Paris was no longer a popular place for American writers to be. The real place for the principal concern of an American writer was thought to be within smelling-distance of the Pittsburgh steelworks or the Chicago stockyards, where the essential business of twentieth-century capitalism was carried out. Living abroad smacked of escapism. For the Left – and in the thirties most writers were on the Left – it was worse. It was a desertion from moral duty.

Yet there continued, nevertheless, to be American writers in Paris. There remained the hard-core Francophiles who had made the city their permanent home such as Gertrude Steine and Natalie Barney. George Rheims, who

Right: Shadow of the Duke taking a picture of his bride.

Above: A Parisian family prepare to go on holiday at government expense. Free holidays were given by the French Government to families with over two children to encourage population growth.

had served as a liaison officer with the French command during the First World War, remained behind to marry a French girl. In his family life and friendships he had become largely Gallicized. He wrote in French so much that his English atrophied to such an extent that he needed a translator to prepare an American edition of one of his novels. Then there was Julien Green. As a boy he had been educated in France. Returning to serve there in the First World War, he decided to remain in Paris and became to all intents and purposes a French writer. As such, he is now one of the Académie Française's *immortels*.

There were even some new arrivals. Paul Bowles came in 1931, to rent a flat above Virgil Thomson's on the Quai Voltaire. He was known at the time, however, as a poet and as a composer rather than as a novelist, and his final place of exile was to be not Paris but Morocco. The least likely of expatriates was the quintessentially thirties novelist James T. Farrell. Farrell never settled into the Parisian atmosphere and his stay in the city was a bitterly unhappy one. He and his wife Dorothy lived close to the starvation level. Soon after Dorothy gave birth to a child in the American Hospital, it died: they did not have the money to have it cremated.

Only one major writer bucked the trend by making Paris his home, and that was the supreme individualist of American letters, Henry Miller. He arrived in 1930, when most of his fellow-countrymen were leaving. He was no callow youth. At 39, he had already passed through a lower-

middle-class German upbringing in Brooklyn and a number of unwanted jobs in New York, of which the longest-lasting had been with the firm he characterized in *Tropic of Capricorn* as the Cosmodemonic Telegraph Company. He had also done a considerable amount of writing, but except for a few short, unnoticed pieces he had gone unpublished.

He had developed something of an obsession about Europe from conversations with immigrants and returned expatriates in New York. He got his first sight of the continent in 1928, on holiday with his second wife, June. On that trip he met Alfred Perlès, an Austrian newspaperman who was subsequently to become one of his closest friends. He was enchanted with what he saw.

When he finally came to stay in Paris, he came without his wife, with very little money, with virtually no knowledge of French and without a working permit. His prospects, as a failed writer approaching middle age, appeared to be nil – there was little chance of his finding work. Yet, oddly enough, the very hopelessness of his situation triggered an explosion of literary creativity that was to produce, in the course of the decade, the best writing of his life. His experience was living proof of the motto he had chosen: "Only get desperate enough and everything will turn out well."

His life style in Paris could hardly have been more

Left: The Duke and Duchess on the Côte d'Azur with their friend and cousin Lord Mountbatten.

different from that of the affluent exiles of the 1920s. In a way it was a throwback to an earlier French artistic tradition, the garret way of life sentimentalized in Henri Murger's *Scènes de la Bohème*. For a bed at nights, he relied either on Montparnasse bughouses or, failing that, on a sofa or mattress in the apartment of a friend. He devised an ingenious solution to the food problem. He drew up a list of fourteen acquaintances, each good for one meal a week, and then informed them, in advance, when they could expect his presence at the lunch or dinner table. If, for one reason or another, a meal was not forthcoming, he had to make do with scraps or else go hungry.

His Paris was no plaything for visitors to toy with; "it is a Paris that has to be lived, that has to be experienced each day in a thousand different forms of torture, a Paris that grows inside you like a cancer, and grows and grows until you are eaten away by it." And yet it was also a place where he found it easy to write. "One needs no artifiical stimulation, in Paris, to create. The atmosphere is saturated with creation."

When things got too difficult, he always managed to find some temporary way of earning a little spending money. He briefly taught English in a barrack-like lycée in Dijon. He wrote publicity material for the Sphinx, a palatial brothel in the boulevard Edgar Quinet to whose opening all the artists of Montparnasse had been invited; the madame liked artists because, she said, she played the violin herself. For his services, Miller earned a few francs and a free frolic with a girl of his choice in one of the Egyptianesque bedrooms. At one stage he even agreed, with some distaste, to pose for pornographic pictures – destined, he was told, for a German private collection. The photographs, which would now have a certain literary curiosity value, have not been seen since.

Above all, he was writing. It was in these hard and

Below: The Royal Gardens in the 1930s.
Right: A traffic jam on the Boulevard Magenta.

Below : Henry Miller, apart from Gertrude Stein, was the
only important American writer to make Paris his home
in the 1930s. The rest departed soon after the
Depression struck.

hopeless days that *Tropic of Cancer* was born. Maybe the hunger had something to do with the heightened, hallucinatory rhetoric of the book. Miller was attempting to set down, with total honesty and without any compromises with conventional respectability, the reality of the life he was leading in Paris. He intended the book to be "a prolonged insult, a gob of spit in the face of Art, a kick in the pants to God, Man, Destiny, Time, Love, Beauty. . ." He expected the book to shock, and shock it did.

It could at that time have been published nowhere but in Paris, and by no-one there but Jack Kahane. This ex-businessman from Manchester, England, had come to Paris specifically to publish the sort of book that could not find a publisher in England or America. He had earlier published Frank Harris's *My Life and Loves* and was later to bring out Lawrence Durrell's *Black Book*. Yet even Kahane was nervous of *Tropic of Cancer*. He sat on it for two years before finally having it printed and even then he distributed it to bookstores with specific instructions that it should not be displayed in shop windows.

By the time that *Tropic of Cancer* was accepted, the worst of Miller's troubles were over. He had found a job, as proofreader on the *Paris Tribune*, which, while less than enthralling, at least provided him steady money. He was able to take an apartment with Alfred Perlès at 4, avenue Anatole France, Clichy – the scene of the adventures later described in his book *Quiet Days in Clichy*. It was the first fixed address he had had since arriving in Paris, and he made the most of it. The spell in Clichy was a happy time of hard work on his new book *Black Spring*, bicycle rides into the countryside, elaborate feasting when money was available, and a great deal of sexual adventuring with girls picked up in local bars or in the big Café Wepler on the place du Clichy.

By this time Miller had gathered a circle of close friends who were to provide him not only with companionship and occasional hospitality, but also with material for his largely autobiographical novels. There was Michael Fraenkel, a Jewish intellectual who had come to Montparnasse after making a lot of money on the New York stock exchange, to write books and to indulge a neurotic obsession with death. There was Fraenkel's crony, Walter Lowenfels, a writer.

Below: The Metro in the 1930s.

Above all, there was Anaïs Nin. A concert pianist's daughter, this talented and beautiful woman, though born in France, was truly international by upbringing. As a child she had travelled around Europe on her father's concert tours; as an adolescent she had lived in New York with her mother, after her parents' separation. By the time that Miller met her she was living in a house in Louveciennes with a walled garden and an interior tastefully furnished in Spanish and Moorish styles. The place became a favorite refuge for Miller. Anaïs was an exquisitely thoughtful hostess. She offered literary conversation as well as an excellent Spanish cuisine. She even took the trouble to select the books left for night-time reading in the guest bedrooms. When Alfred Perlès arrived with his current girlfriend, "a young slut of fifteen, though she pretended to be eighteen", he found that the books chosen included *Peter Pan*, *Alice in Wonderland* and the Marquis de Sade's *120 Days of Sodom*.

The last five years of Miller's Paris residence were spent in a cul-de-sac in the Alésia district called the Villa Seurat. By then *Tropic of Cancer* had appeared, and he no longer needed a steady job to provide him with an income. He also had a growing underground literary reputation. His most enthusiastic admirer was Lawrence Durrell, who on the strength of his admiration came with his wife from their home on Corfu to join Miller in Paris.

The Villa Seurat years were some of the happiest of Miller's life. While most of Europe was worrying over economic problems and the approach of war, he was enjoying himself with Rabelaisian gusto. He worked on *Tropic of Capricorn* and other books, but also found the time to indulge in some pure examples of literary high spirits. When Alfred Perlès lost his job with the closing of the *Chicago Tribune* Paris edition, he published at his own expense a pamphlet entilted *What are you going to do about Alf?* urging his readers to provide his friend with enough cash to finish off a novel on Ibiza. Another private publication was entitled *Money and How it Gets that Way*. This was purely and simply a practical joke, inspired by a challenge

to write a serious-sounding treatise on economics that would make no sense at all. It netted an interested note of thanks from the Governor of the Bank of England.

The high kinks at the Villa Seurat culminated in Alfred Perlès's editorship of the journal of the American Country Club of France – *The Booster*. Perlès had been hired as publicity manager of the club, a job for which he was totally unsuited. He was soon fired, but the club's owner left him with full editorial control over *The Booster* as a parting present.

He little realized what he had let himself in for. Perlès and his friends drew up an editorial board for the magazine that included virtually the entire Villa Seurat circle. Henry Miller, Lawrence Durrell and William Saroyan were appointed Literary Editors. Anaïs Nin was Society Editor. Henry Miller appeared again in the unlikely role of Fashion Editor. Michael Fraenkel was listed under 'Department of Metaphysics and Metempsychosis'. Walter Lowenfels was mysteriously made responsible for 'Butter News'.

Surprisingly enough, the club's owner was quite pleased with their first issue. He was only a little perplexed by the editorial, an explanation of the *Booster* philosophy that ended on a note of elevated optimism: "We leave the dirty work of making the world over to the quacks who specialize in such matters. For us things are all right as they are. In fact, everything is excellent – including the high-grade bombers with ice-boxes and what not. We wish everybody well and no gravel in the kidneys."

It was unconventional stuff for a golf-club magazine, but hardly shocking. The real trouble came with the second issue. This contained a retelling of an Eskimo legend about the taking of a beautiful young maiden by an old bachelor, who at the climactic moment is sucked bodily into the girl, to re-emerge later as a skeleton. This was too much for the clubhouse. Perlès was warned that he would be sued if the Country Club's name was mentioned in future issues.

The Booster survived for only one more issue – "The Air-Conditioned Womb Number" – but was subsequently reborn as *Delta*. Under its new name it continued to refuse to take the contemporary world seriously on its own tragic terms. An issue appearing immediately after the Munich Crisis was entitled "Special Peace and Dismemberment Number with Jitterbug-Shag Requiem", and its cover was adorned with a black border, like a funeral announcement.

Yet the rest of the world could only be ignored up to a certain point. The pressure of outside events finally penetrated even the charmed circle of the Villa Seurat. By 1939 it was increasingly obvious that Czechoslovakia had not satisfied Hitler's appetite for expansion, and that war was coming sooner or later. Miller's *Tropic of Capricorn* was by that time ready for publication. He received a sizeable advance for the book from his publisher, Jack Kahane and with that money decided to leave France and to accompany Lawrence Durrell back to Corfu for a long-planned Greek excursion. It was an apt and fitting conclusion to the playful interlude of his Paris days that they should end with his going on holiday while the rest of the word was preparing to go to war.

Left: Celebrations in a small café on July 14th.
Right: Fishing along the Seine was still popular.

Below: Traffic snarls and their accompaniment by claxons became part of Paris life in the 1930s, like this one at the corner of rue Cadet and rue Lafayette.

Right: A vendor of hot chestnuts.
Below: Sidewalk cafés lost some of their vivacity in the thirties.

Right: Cabarets which catered to remaining rich foreigners and wealthy French carried on in the thirties, but tables were more easy to find.
Below: The Café de la Paix frequented by Americans on the Place de l'Opéra did not suffer a great loss of custom.

Below left: The Institut de France along the Seine in 1935.
Below: A working class mother's day at the 'beach' was a dip in the Seine for her small children.

Below: Miss Venus of 1936 was crowned at a Paris music hall after a fiercely contested competition.

Above : Models of the atelier 'Jenny' on the Champs Elysées in 1930.
Right : The second lady on the right, Miss Claude May, won the first prize in the bathing suit competition in 1936 at the Piscine Molitor in Auteuil despite all efforts of others to win.
Below : Entrance to the Métro at the Gare du Nord.

9. Occupation and Liberation

On August 31, 1939, Elsa Maxwell, who had returned to France from America earlier that summer, threw a housewarming party. A wealthy American couple she knew had given her a villa above Cannes, a sizeable place that commanded a magnificent view over the Riviera coastline and the Mediterranean beyond. Some 200 guests turned up to help her celebrate her new acquisition.

The mood, however, was not very festive. The guests were apprehensive and ill at ease. Hitler's invasion of Poland was in everyone's mind, and the gaiety was muted. Suddenly, from the terrace, they noticed something strange happening in the valley below them. All along the coast, from Cap d'Antibes to the Esterel, the lights began to go out. The entire coastline was plunged into darkness as they watched. They soon realized what it meant. Someone had ordered a blackout. The War had started.

The time for parties was over. Elsa Mazwell and most non-resident Americans left the country immediately. Yet in the first eight months of the war in France, nothing very much happened. It was the period the French call the *drôle de guerre* ('funny kind of war'). In Paris and the other cities the streets were unusually empty, and most of the people left in them were either over military age or else very young. The blackout was enforced, and the dim blue lights that lit the streets at night gave them a sinister aspect. A few commodities were rationed, but there were no real food shortages. Gas masks had been issued, and people were expected to carry them in the street. But there were no large-scale air-raids. Nor was there any fighting in France. The whole country was waiting.

In view of the atmosphere of calm, the reactions of American residents in France were mixed. The American Embassy advised repatriation and even chartered some boats to ease the run on tickets for the transatlantic liners ordered by those who did not believe in sticking it out to the last moment. But many others provisionally decided to stay,

Left: Wehrmacht troops enter Paris in June 1940.
Below: Maurice Chevalier and Josephine Baker are acclaimed by *poilus* after entertaining them in 1939.

Above: German soldiers shout 'Heil, General' to their
Commanding Officer in the parade on the Place de la
Concorde in June 1940.
Right: Bicycled troops continue the parade, witnessed
by only a handful of French citizens.
Far right: The swastika over the Chamber of Deputies
and signposts indicate the way to the 'New Order'.

hoping that, as in the First World War, the greater part of
France would remain outside the combat zone.

They were soon to be disillusioned. When the blow came
it was swift and sudden. Hitler invaded France and the Low
Countries on May 10, 1940, and by the end of the month it
was apparent that Paris was likely to fall to the Germans.
The city's inhabitants had very little time in which to
stomach the unpalatable truth, but the facts of the situation
were only too apparent. A constant stream of Belgian
refugees was already passing southwards through the city.
Soon the Parisians were following them. The mass civilian
exodus began.

As the Germans approached Paris, the escape routes
began to clog up. The major roads out of the city were soon
blocked by cars that had been abandoned by their owners
after running out of gas. Outside the railway stations
would-be travellers camped out all night in the hope of
obtaining tickets for a south-bound train. There were a few
Americans among the refugees. Josephine Baker managed
to reach her chateau in the Dordogne. Virgil Thomson
took temporary refuge with friends in the Pyrenees. Man
Ray had less luck; driving south towards Bordeaux, he
found himself in the occupied zone at the time the Armistice
was signed on June 25 and had to return to Paris.

CHAMBRE DES DEPUTES
Der Militärbefehlshaber in Frankreich
O.Qu West
Rue d'Astorg 25-27
Kommandant von Gross-Paris
Platzkommandantur
Place de l'Opéra 2
Wehrwirtschafts- u. Rüstungsstab Frankreich
Luftwaffen-Lazarett
Paris-Clichy
General der Luftwaffe Paris
Rue du Faubourg St. Honoré 52
Deutsches Rotes Kreuz
Fort Charenton
Fort Bicêtre
Gemüse
Quai d'Austerlitz
Sanitätspark
Fort de Vanves
Clamart
Boulevard de l'Hôpital
Av. de Choisy 158
Chem. Untersuchungsstelle
beim. Mil.-Befhb. in Frankreich.
39 BIS, Rue de Dantzig
WH-TANKSTELLE
für Einzelfahrzeuge
GL/Paris
Lw. Lazarett Paris
Abt. MEUDON
Nächste GFP. Dienststelle
Avenue Duquesne 5

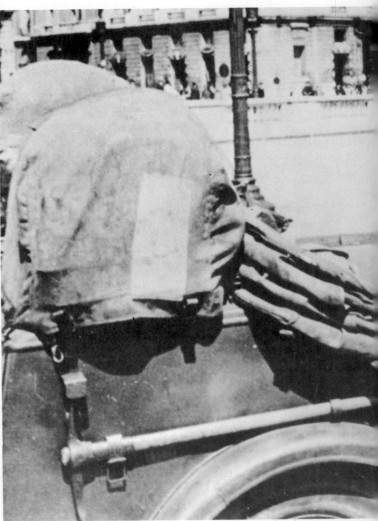

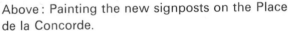
Above: Painting the new signposts on the Place
de la Concorde.

The terms of the Armistice created three separate zones
in France. There was a forbidden military zone in the *Nord*
department; an occupied zone, administered directly by the
Germans from Paris, and covering essentially the north-
western half of the country; and a 'free' zone in the south-
east half, under the control of the collaborationist government based in Vichy. A kind of normalcy returned to France
and the refugees slowly began to make their way home.

Americans, as nationals of a neutral country, were not
subject to any special harassment in either the occupied or
unoccupied zones. Like all other civilians, however, they
needed special authorization to travel. Those who wished to
return home could no longer do so from France, as the
transatlantic service had come to a halt. With the Nazis
occupying the entire western seaboard of Europe from the
north of Norway to the Spanish frontier, the only route back
ran through neutral Portugal. Ships still sailed to New York
at irregular intervals from Lisbon.

Among the Americans to make use of the Lisbon route
back to America were Virgil Thomson and Man Ray, who
sailed on the same boat, the *Excalibur*, in the company of
Salvador Dali and the film-maker René Clair. Robert
McAlmon was also to use it for his final return to America.
He knew by then that he was suffering from tuberculosis.

He had lost most of his literary ambitions, and went to work
for his brother's businesses in El Paso. He spent the last
years of his life in clinics, first in Mexico, then at Desert Hot
Springs, California, where he lived alone and almost
totally forgotten until his death in 1956, at the age of 59.

Only a very few Americans decided to sit the war out in
occupied Europe. Natalie Barney and Romaine Brooks
retired to a villa outside Florence. Ezra Pound was also in
Italy throughout the war. His growing obsession with the
economic theories of Social Credit had led him to support
actively Mussolini's regime. During the war he made, at his
own suggestion, a number of rambling, semi-coherent and
markedly anti-semitic broadcasts for the Italian state radio
system. The broadcasts smacked more of the crank than the
quisling, but after the war, Pound was forced to spend long
years in a Washington insane asylum to expiate their
memory.

While Ezra Pound was collaborating with Fascism in
Italy, Josephine Baker, first in France and then in North
Africa, was doing everything in her power to combat its
German equivalent. As a French citizen through her first
marriage, she rallied early but covertly to the Free French
cause. She agreed to act as a cover for the agent responsible
for contacts between the French Resistance and the
British intelligence services. The agent, a former head of
French military counter-espionage, masqueraded as
Josephine's secretary. Her foreign tours provided him with

opportunities to contact British agents. In this manner, details of German troop disposition in western France and of the Nazi spy network in Great Britain were carried from France to Lisbon, written in invisible ink on the scores of Josephine's hit songs.

In 1941 she left France for North Africa, where she was to remain for the rest of the war. For the better part of two years she was laid up by illness: first peritonitis, then paratyphoid. After her recovery she gave a series of concerts in North Africa and the Middle East in aid of the Free French Forces. She was rewarded with the Croix de Lorraine, presented to her at a gala performance by General de Gaulle in person, and was granted the rank of sub-lieutenant in the Free French Army.

As a mulatto, Josephine Baker had particular reason to dislike the racial theories of Nazism. So did Gertrude Stein and Alice B. Toklas, as Jews. Yet they remained in France throughout the Occupation. It could have proved a foolhardy decision. Had they been denounced to the German authorities, they might well have shared the fate of the French poet Max Jacob, who, despite the fact that he had long been a convert to Catholicism and was living a life of contemplation under the protection of a community of Benedictine monks, was sent to the Drancy concentration camp, where he died of pneumonia.

In fact, the couple made not one decision to remain, but a series of decisions. The question first came up at Bilignin,

Above: Wehrmacht soldiers read their 'local' newspaper on the Place de la Concorde.

where they were staying at the outbreak of the war. They decided to await events there, in the hope that the war would soon be over. They got travel permits for a short visit to Paris, to collect their papers and winter clothing. They left the paintings on the walls of the rue Christine apartment, for want of anywhere else to put them, taking only the Picasso portrait of Gertrude Stein and Cézanne's *Portrait of Hortense* back to Bilignin with them.

In 1940, during the German invasion, they again thought of leaving. However, before they could make up their minds whether to head for Bordeaux, Spain or Switzerland, the Armistice was signed, and they discovered that their region was in the unoccupied zone. This again calmed their fears, and they settled down once more to a quiet and economical life of work and reflection, supporting themselves on the produce from their vegetable garden and the rare food available in the local shops.

Oddly enough, Gertrude Stein was an ardent admirer of Marshal Pétain. At one stage she even started to translate a volume of his speeches with a view to publishing them in America. The reasons for her admiration were largely selfish; as she put it, "I always thought he was right to make the armistice, in the first place it was more comfortable for us who were here." She had some friends among the Vichy

intelligentsia, whose influence helped protect her from persecution. The most notable was Bernard Fäy, who had been put in control of the Bibliothèque Nationale. After the war, Gertrude Stein tried to repay her debt to him by pleading his cause in Paris when he was charged with collaborating. Despite her intervention, he was imprisoned.

The situation got worse after German troops moved into unoccupied France in November, 1942. Gertrude and Alice even lost the house at Bilignin, which was reclaimed by its owner, a demobilized French Army captain. Gertrude was sufficiently upset by this turn of events to risk starting two separate law suits against the owner. She was mollified when friends found a new home for Alice and her a few miles away in the village of Culoz. At that moment they were probably closer to denunciation than at any other time in the war.

Their problems by no means ended with the discovery of the new house. There were flurries of excitement when first a German major, then a contingent of Italian soldiers, were billeted on them. The couple were also hard-pressed financially, and the Cézanne portrait had to be sold. A few weeks after the sale, the designer Pierre Balmain, who had taken refuge in nearby Aix-les-Bains, was invited to dinner. Noticing that the portrait was missing from its normal place, he asked where it had gone. Gertrude answered ruefully, "We are eating the Cézanne."

The mystery of their apparent immunity from persecution was only cleared up after the troops of the French Resistance regained control of the Ain in 1944. She and Alice had been the beneficiaries of a conspiracy of silence conducted on their behalf by the public functionaries responsible for Bilignin and Culoz, who had simply failed to inscribe their names on the list of Jewish residents required by the occupying authorities. As the Mayor of Culoz explained to her: "You are obviously too old for life in a concentration camp. You would not survive it, so why should I tell them?"

As it turned out, Stein had a less troubled time during the Occupation than her sixth-arrondissement compatriot, Sylvia Beach, whose conduct after the arrival of the Germans was marked by determined Yankee stubbornness and courage. She rejected all the appeals made to her by the American Embassy to leave Paris, and insisted on keeping Shakespeare and Company open. She also refused to get rid of her Jewish friend, Françoise Bernheim, who by Nazi race laws was forced to wear a large yellow Star of David. Sylvia made a point of sharing the restrictions placed upon her friend which included not being able to enter public places, such as cafés or cinemas, nor even to sit on public benches.

Left: Nazi troops enjoyed the city. Their treatment of civilians was cool and correct initially.
Below: The Americans returned to Paris in August 1944.

Shakespeare and Company eventually had to be closed after an angry German major had threatened to confiscate its goods. Its owner cleared it totally within two hours, hiding the books in an empty apartment above the shop, taking out the shelves and light fittings and painting out the shop sign.

By this time America was in the war and Sylvia was officially classed as an enemy alien. She was eventually arrested, and spent six months in an internment camp. When released on the understanding that she could be reinterned at any time, she decided to go underground, hiding in an American-run student hotel that benefited from a partial immunity from German interference through the protection of the University of Paris.

She also kept in touch with her friend Adrienne Monnier, whose bookshop in the rue de l'Odéon she visited almost daily. She was in fact staying with Adrienne at the time of the Liberation when the first American detachments reached Paris. So it was that one morning she heard a column of jeeps draw up outside the shop, and an American voice boom "Sylvia!" from the street outside. She rushed downstairs to be swept up into the arms of her old admirer, Ernest Hemingway, who as a war correspondent for Collier's Magazine, had been among the first Americans to reach Paris.

Left: Parisian girls greeted the Americans enthusiastically.
Below: GIs are welcomed on Liberation Day.

American soldiers were back in Paris, and Hemingway had been reunited with Sylvia Beach. A familiar image of the city seemed to be forming, like the picture in a jigsaw puzzle, from elements that had long been dispersed and scattered. Another piece was added when Gertrude Stein and Alice Toklas arrived back safely from Culoz. They found that their apartment in the rue Christine had been altered, but that the picture collection was intact. They subsequently learned that two Gestapo men had broken in. A secretary who lived on the floor below overheard them reviling the paintings as 'decadent filth'. She had the good sense to call the local police commissariat. A couple of gendarmes were sent round to ask the Germans to leave, and, providentially, the paintings were saved from harm. Stein's 'guests' even left a thank-you note.

Paris was free once more, and its beauty had survived the war intact. Yet the sense of time regained felt by returning Americans in the first joy of the Liberation was not lasting. Things had changed, people were older, and the prewar scene was not to recreate itself. Though she continued to live in Paris until her death, Sylvia Beach was never again to run a bookstore. Hemingway returned to America shortly after the Allies entered Germany. Gertrude Stein, the doyenne of them all, did not long survive the Allied victory. She died in a hospital operating theater in 1946. It was a merciful release; the fatal operation revealed that she was suffering from an incurable cancer. With Gertrude Stein an era died. Paris was still Paris, but it was not the same.

Above left and right: Gertrude Stein greets Sergeant
Robert Ashley who made a film of her 'adventures' in
France after her return to Paris. Her flat was occupied by
German officers during the war, and much to her
surprise none of her valuable collection of paintings
was taken. In fact, a note of thanks was left by her
'guests'.
Above: The Stars and Stripes is carried in triumph
through a Paris street on August 25, 1944.

With the passing of the older generation something died in Paris; but fresh, though different roots, had already been put down to replace it. The atmosphere was very different in 1945 from that of 1920. The experience of occupation and of resistance had left scars that were not to heal completely for a quarter of a century. An existential awareness, based on a tragic sense of human commitment, had replaced the joyful nihilism of the twenties. The city was as animated as before but the center of activity was now in the bars and cellars of St. Germain, not the expatriate Montparnasse cafés.

Yet beneath it all Paris itself had not changed. Great cities do not change; like great trees, they only grow and develop. Returning exiles complained that it was not the city they had known, for the faces were different and old habits had been forgotten. But for fresh generations of visiting Americans, Paris waited to be discovered anew, as rich and marvelous as ever.

Below: Janet Flanner and Ernest Hemingway at the Deux Magots in the autumn of 1944.
Right: Hemingway and Gary Cooper on the Champs Elysées after the war, remembering things past.
Bottom: Hemingway was a war correspondent in France in 1944-45.
Overleaf: An American military band on the Place de la Concorde. *Plus ça change . . .*

Index

Picture Credits